WATERLILY FIRE
Poems 1935–1962

ɚ WATERLILY FIRE
Poems 1935–1962 ɚ

Muriel Rukeyser

THE MACMILLAN COMPANY   NEW YORK

Macmillan New York, London
A Division of The Crowell-Collier Publishing Company
1962 ɚ

৪৯ ACKNOWLEDGMENTS

For permission to publish the poems in the last part of this book, I wish to acknowledge the kindness of the following magazines: *Poetry, The Vassar Review, American Judaism*. These publishers have granted permission to print poems which first appeared in books: New Directions, Harper & Brothers, Simon & Schuster, Inc. This selection was made from the following books: *Theory of Flight, U.S.I., A Turning Wind, Beast in View, The Green Wave, Elegies, Selected Poems, One Life, Body of Waking*. This volume is published by arrangement with New Directions.

First Printing

The Macmillan Company, New York
Brett-Macmillan Ltd., Galt, Ontario

Printed in the United States of America

Library of Congress catalog card number: 62-13595

DESIGNED BY RON FARBER

ॐ My thanks to MARIE DE L. WELCH and to M. L. ROSENTHAL
—both poets, critics, friends—who helped me select the poems
in this book. ॐ

ᕿ CONTENTS

I.
From THEORY OF FLIGHT

• EFFORT AT SPEECH
BETWEEN TWO PEOPLE •

: Speak to me.   Take my hand.   What are you now?
 I will tell you all.   I will conceal nothing.
 When I was three, a little child read a story about a rabbit
 who died, in the story, and I crawled under a chair :
 a pink rabbit : it was my birthday, and a candle
 burnt a sore spot on my finger, and I was told to be happy.

: Oh, grow to know me.   I am not happy.   I will be open:
 Now I am thinking of white sails against a sky like music,
 like glad horns blowing, and birds tilting, and an arm about me.
 There was one I loved, who wanted to live, sailing.

: Speak to me.   Take my hand.   What are you now?
 When I was nine, I was fruitily sentimental,
 fluid : and my widowed aunt played Chopin,
 and I bent my head on the painted woodwork, and wept.
 I want now to be close to you.   I would
 link the minutes of my days close, somehow, to your days.

: I am not happy.   I will be open.
 I have liked lamps in evening corners, and quiet poems.
 There has been fear in my life.   Sometimes I speculate
 On what a tragedy his life was, really.

: Take my hand.   Fist my mind in your hand.   What are
        you now?
 When I was fourteen, I had dreams of suicide,
 and I stood at a steep window, at sunset, hoping toward death :
 if the light had not melted clouds and plains to beauty,
 if light had not transformed that day, I would have leapt.
 I am unhappy.   I am lonely.   Speak to me.

: I will be open.   I think he never loved me:
 he loved the bright beaches, the little lips of foam

3 •

that ride small waves, he loved the veer of gulls:
he said with a gay mouth: I love you.   Grow to know me.

/ : What are you now?   If we could touch one another,
if these our separate entities could come to grips,
clenched like a Chinese puzzle . . . yesterday
I stood in a crowded street that was live with people,
and no one spoke a word, and the morning shone.
Everyone silent, moving. . . . Take my hand.   Speak to me.

❧ BREATHING LANDSCAPE ❧

Lying in the sun
and lying here so still
an egg might slowly hatch in this still hand.

The people pass
abruptly they nod : they smile
trailed in the air, silence follows their faces.

I know, lying
how the hills are fixed
and the day-moon runs at the head of the fixed hills.

Nothing crossed the field
all day but a bird
skirting the tall grass in briefest transit.

Their stern ideas
are a long work to each
and even armored we hardly touch each other.

The wind leans,
the air placed formally
about these faces and thoughts in formal dance.

Silence hangs in the air.
Nothing speaks but the sound
of certain rivers continuing underground.

৯ SAND-QUARRY
WITH MOVING FIGURES ৯

Father and I drove to the sand-quarry across the ruined marsh-
    lands,
miles of black grass, burned for next summer's green.
I reached my hand to his beneath the lap-robe,
we looked at the stripe of fire, the blasted scene.

"It's all right," he said, "they can control the flames,
on one side men are standing, and on the other the sea;"
but I was terrified of stubble and waste of black
and his ugly villages he built and was showing me.

The countryside turned right and left about the car,
straight through October we drove to the pit's heart;
sand, and its yellow canyon and standing pools
and the wealth of the split country set us farther apart.
"Look," he said, "this quarry means rows of little houses,
stucco and a new bracelet for you are buried there;"
but I remembered the ruined patches, and I saw the land ruined,
exploded, burned away, and the fiery marshes bare.

"We'll own the countryside, you'll see how soon I will,
you'll have acres to play in" : I saw the written name
painted on stone in the face of the steep hill:
"That's your name, Father!"   "And yours!" he shouted, laugh-
    ing.
"No, Father, no!"   He caught my hand as I cried,
and smiling, entered the pit, ran laughing down its side.

ᘿ SONG FOR DEAD CHILDREN ᘿ

We set great wreaths of brightness on the graves of the passionate
who required tribute of hot July flowers :
for you, O brittle-hearted, we bring offering
remembering how your wrists were thin and your delicate bones
    not yet braced for conquering.

The sharp cries of ghost-boys are keen above the meadows,
the little girls continue graceful and wondering;
flickering evening on the lakes recalls those young
heirs whose developing years have sunk to earth
    their strength not tested, their praise unsung.

Weave grasses for their childhood : who will never see
love or disaster or take sides against decay
balancing the choices of maturity;
silent and coffin'd in silence while we pass
    loud in defiance of death, the helpless lie.

ᘿ NOTES FOR A POEM ᘿ

Here are the long fields inviolate of thought,
here are the planted fields raking the sky,
signs in the earth :
water-cast shuttles of light flickering the underside of rock.
These have been shown before; but the fields know new hands,
the son's fingers grasp warmly at the father's hoe ;
there will be new ways of seeing these ancestral lands.

    "In town, the munitions plant has been poor since the war,
    And nothing but a war will make it rich again."
    Holy, holy, holy, sings the church next door.

Time-ridden, a man strides the current of a stream's flowing,
stands, flexing the wand curvingly over his head,
tracking the water's prism with the flung line.
Summer becomes productive and mature.
Farmers watch tools like spikes of doom against the sure
condemning sky descending upon the hollow lands.

> The water is ridged in muscles on the rock,
> force for the State is planted in the stream-bed.
> Water springs from the stone—the State is fed.

Morning comes, brisk with light,
a broom of color over the threshold.
Long flights of shadows escape to the white sky :
a spoon is straightened.   Day grows.   The sky is blued.
The water rushes over the shelves of stone
to anti-climax on the mills below the drop.
The planted fields are bright and rake the sky.
Power is common.   Earth is grown
and overgrown in unrelated strength, the moral
rehearsed already, often.
(There must be the gearing of these facts
into coördination, in a poem or numbers,
rows of statistics, or the cool iambs.)
The locked relationships which will be found
are a design to build these factual timbers—
a plough of thought to break this stubborn ground.

❧ WOODEN SPRING ❧

How horrible late spring is, with the full death of the frozen
    tight bulbs
brownly rotting in earth;   and each chord of light
rayed into slivers, a bunch of grapes plucked grape by grape apart,
a warm chord broken into the chilled single notes.

(Let us rely on cerebral titillation
for the red stimulus of sensuous supply;)
here is no heat, no fierce color : spring is no bacchante this year
eager to celebrate her carnal dedication.

The ghosts swim, lipless, eyeless, upward :
the crazy hands point in five directions down :
to the sea, the high ridge, the bush, the blade, the weak white
    root :
thumping at life in an agony of birth, abortive fruit.

Spring is very mad for greenness now
(: I suppose it would be beautiful, if we let ourselves be :),
but we must strip nascent earth bare of green mystery.
Trees do not grow high as skyscrapers in my town,

and flowers not so lovely as the pale bewildered youth,
hands pointing in five directions upward and out;
and spring in the fields and cities spreads to the north and south,
and is comforted in desire for the sun's mouth.

Earth does not seem wooden to the comforted spring :
(spring could not seem so dull, I comforted :
but there must be abstraction, where fields need not sprout, waves
    pound,
there must be silence where no rushing grasses sound,
life in this lack of death, comfort on this wide ground).

ৡ SONNET ৡ

My thoughts through yours refracted into speech
transmute this room musically tonight,
the notes of contact flowing, rhythmic, bright
with an informal art beyond my single reach.
Outside, dark birds fly in a greening time :
wings of our sistered wishes beat these walls :
and words afflict our minds in near footfalls
approaching with a latening hour's chime.

And if an essential thing has flown between us,
rare intellectual bird of communication,
let us seize it quickly;   let our preference
choose it instead of softer things to screen us
each from the other's self : muteness or hesitation,
nor petrify live miracle by our indifference.

ৡ FOUR IN A FAMILY ৡ

The father and mother sat, and the sister beside her.
I faced the two women across the table's width,
speaking, and all the time he looked at me,
sorrowing, saying nothing, with his hard tired breath.

Their faces said : This is your home;   and I :
I never come home, I never go away.
And they all answered : Stay.

All day the city turned about this room,
and silence had remained between our faces,
divisions outside to concentrate a world
tally here only to dead profits and losses.

9 ৡ

We follow barrier voices, and we go fast,
unknown to each other, they race, I turn away.
No voice is strong enough to cry me Stay.

My sister, I wished upon you those delights
time never buries,
more precious than heroes.

Strange father, strange mother, who are you, who are you?
Where have I come,
how shall I prosper home?

ৡৈ THE GYROSCOPE ৡৈ

But this is our desire, and of its worth. . . .
Power electric-clean, gravitating outward at all points,
moving in savage fire, fusing all durable stuff
but never itself being fused with any force
homing in no hand nor breast nor sex
for buried in these lips we rise again,
bent over these plans, our faces raise to see.
Direct spears are shot outward from the conscience
fulfilling what far circuits?   Orbit of thought
what axis do you lean on, what strictnesses evade
impelled to the long curves of the will's ambition?
Centrifugal power, expanding universe
within expanding universe, what stillnesses
lie at your center resting among motion?
Study communications, looking inward, find what traffic
you may have with your silences : looking outward, survey
what you have seen of places :
                              many times this week I seemed
          to hear you speak my name
                              how you turn the flatnesses
     of your cheek and will not hear my words
                              then reaching the given latitude

and longitude, we searched for the ship and found nothing
                    and, gentlemen, shall we define desire
    including every impulse toward psychic progress?
Roads are cut into the earth leading away from our place
at the inevitable hub.   All directions are **out,**
all desire turns outward : we, introspective,
continuing to find in ourselves the microcosm
imaging continents, powers, relations, reflecting
all history in a bifurcated Engine.
Here is the gyroscope whirling out pulsing in tides illimitably
                    widening, live force contained
in a sphere of rigid boundary;   concentrate
at the locus of all forces, spinning with black speed
revolving outward perpetually, turning with its torque
all the developments of the secret will.
Flaming origins were our fathers in the heat of the earth,
pushing to the crust, water and sea-flesh,
undulant tentacles ingrown on the ocean's floor,
frondy anemones and scales' armor gave us birth.
Bring us to air, ancestors! and we breathed
the young flesh wincing against naked December.
Masters of fire, fire gave us riches, gave us life.
Masters of water, water gave us riches, gave us life,
masters of earth, earth gave us riches, gave us life.
Air mocks, and desire whirls outward in strict frenzy, leaping,
elastic circles widening from the mind,
turning constricted to the mind again.
The dynamics of desire are explained
in terms of action outward and reaction to a core
obscured and undefined, except, perhaps, as "God in Heaven,"
    "God in Man,"
Elohim intermittent with the soul, recurrent
as Father and Holy Ghost, Word and responsive Word,
merging with contact in continual sunbursts,
the promise, the response, the hands laid on,
the hammer swung to the anvil, mouth fallen on mouth,
the plane nose up into an open sky.
Roads are cut, purchase is gained on our wish,
the turbines gather momentum, tools are given :

whirl in desire, hurry to ambition, return,
maintaining the soul's polarity;　　be : fly.

৯৺ SUNDAYS, THEY SLEEP LATE ৯৺

The days are incestuous, each with its yesterday,
and they, walking heavily in the streets, atone for the moment's
sin : their memories laboring under the weight of today
in its perverse alliance with the past.　　Laments

are heard, droning from the city on all other mornings
but Sundays, they sleep late, and need not cry to wake,
sniffling in the pillow, realizing the day's churnings
of minute resolving to minute, and the whole day slack,

of wind bled of vigor, the talk in the parlor
of people pasturing on each other's minds, and sunset
evolving in the air, a quiet change against the duller
signs in pandemonium of day's gradual transit:

the klaxon voices through the roads, the picnickers joking
(returning from the fields), who wept before they dressed.
On Sundays their dreams are longer, and their waking
is a long exhalation of their weeks, decompressed.

There are these things to be remembered : the nine boys waiting,
battle-fronts of the rising army with holes bitten by death,
the man in the prison overland, and history beating
out the recurrent facts of power, suppression, wrath.

The days are incestuous.　　They witness the daily binding
of minutes linking backwards.　　Their remembering atones
in no part for the things they remember.　　They sink in blinding
sleep too long, they dissolve in sleep their remembering bones.

THE SURROUNDED

They escape before, but their shadows walk behind,
filling the city with formidable dark,
spilling black over the sun's run gold, speeding a rumor
of warfare and the sciences of death, and work
of treason and exposure, following
me for an easy mark.

The sky is travelled by brightness, clouds ignite,
flame is incised upon the martyred air;
the city dissolves in foaming craters, stars
falling in multitudes dazzle the sky with fire,
and I pursue them, I am pursued, and
they are everywhere.

Now there is no more brightness, and no shadow
but the shadow of a thought, and I'm in jail enough
to know conviction with prisoner certainty,
haunted by protest, lacking completion's proof
surrounded by shadows
more plausible than love.

MOVIE   130327

Spotlight her face   her face has no light in it
touch the cheek with light   inform the eyes
press meanings on those lips.

                    See cities from the air,
fix a cloud in the sky, one bird in the bright air,
one perfect mechanical flower in her hair.

Make your young men ride over the mesquite plains;
produce our country on film : here are the flaming shrubs,

the Negroes put up their hands in Hallelujahs,
the young men balance at the penthouse door.
We focus on the screen : look   they tell us
you are a nation of similar whores   remember the Maine
remember you have a democracy of champagne ——

And slowly the female face kisses the young man,
over his face the twelve-foot female head
the yard-long mouth enlarges and yawns

                                        The End

Here is a city   here the village grows
here are the rich men standing rows on rows,
but the crowd seeps behind the cowboy the lover the king,
past the constructed sets America rises
the bevelled classic doorways   the alleys of trees are witness
America rises in a wave a mass
pushing away the rot.

                    The Director cries Cut!
hoarsely CUT   and the people send pistons of force
crashing against the CUT! CUT! of the straw men.

Light is superfluous upon these eyes,
across our minds push new portents of strength
destroying the sets, the flat faces, the mock skies.

੩੦ CATS AND A COCK ੩੦

                              for Eleanor Clark
What hill can ever hold us?
                    Standing high
we saw December packed, snow upon snow,
empty until the cars, leaping in beams below,
opened the shadow of the trees in fans

enormous on the plain, fragile and magnified.
Print of the delicate branch sweeping our feet
in hundred hugeness, passing to white again.

Up the dark hill a pack of cats :
bursting from hollows, streaming to the crest,
streaming all night toward dawn
when green invaded east.
We stood to hear the rigid cock cry Five
a black cock crowing over cold water,
when all those cats found their sole proud objective
and whirled away to slaughter.

. . . . .

We walk the streets
of the dark city
placards at back
light in our heads,

Moon rides over us
town streams below :
Strike and support us
the strike-songs go.

Ceilings of stars
disturb our faces,
tantrums of light
summon our eyes;

The daystar stands
hungry for day :
we file, regarding
this twin morning.

Shall that bind us,
parade and planet,
mobile and point?
No, not yet,

15 ॐ

                    there is labor
                    before a reunion.
                    Poets, pickets,
                    prepare for dawn!

                    .   .   .   .   .

Come chop the days
lop off the moving hours,
we had not known there were disparate things.

Forget these syntheses and fade
peerless and distant into a distant grave
still hoping unity indeed be made?

I wish you to be saved . . . you wish . . . he wishes . . . she . . .
in conjugation of a destiny.
We were figures rubbed by wind passing upon a frieze,
galloping figures at a column's base
hungrily running from death and marble space.

I give you cats : I give you a cock on a hill :
these stream in beauty : that stands blocked in pride
I pledge you death until
they fight and acquiesce, or one has died.

Earnestly and slowly I continue :
no one could guess how the impact of a word
heard plain and plainly understood
can have attacked us so and so deferred.

Fight them down, deliver yourself, friend!
see, we all fight it down : poetry, picket-line,
to master pride and muscle fluid with sun,
conflicting graces moving to one end.

                    .   .   .   .   .

Witness the unfailing war, season with season,
license and principle, sex with tortured sex,
class versus class, and help us to survey
this city for faces, this hill for tracks.

Sickness will bind itself upon our tissue
clipping off with restriction blood and heat and milk,
becoming real against all disbelief
a sly ghost coughing to advertise its bulk.

Climax to Egypt, our milestone pyramid
forces out history and we remember
conflict of thousands of April processions,
rival winds ripping at the heart's deep chamber.

No natural poison : a vicious, banker's thrust
nudges toward dissolution during war,
this peak of open battle points disgust
of decay, counterattacks backing us to our door.

This is when death thrives in the rot
and formal nightmare, zebra of sleep,
presents us madness, diffusion to remember,
to cherish, loss if we lose; and dust to keep.

Resent the nightmare, assume a waking stance,
this clock of revolt, held in the hand and striking,
clapping, the violent wings of a struck bird,
speaks your top hour, marks your fatal chance.

.   .   .   .   .

"Still elegiac! : between two battles, when one is happy
to be alive !"—Rosa Luxemburg

Here was a battle forced by the brain's fortitude,
mapping machines of peace before crisis had come;
and by this planning we create a world
new-hearted, secure from common delirium.

If the strike was won, the prisoners freed at last,
the cataract tapped for power, parade-songs sung :
Prepare for continuance, open your brilliant love,
your life, — front April, give it tongue !

.   .   .   .   .

Below the flowering hedge
rest in the light, forget
grief's awful violet
and indecision's wedge
driven into your pride,
and how the past has died.

Here is transition :
pain, but no surgeon's knife
: anaesthetize your life?
you lose the vision
of how you simply walk
toward a younger folk,

simply, a flaming wire
advancing on the night,
reducing midnight
to clear noon-fire ;
moving upon the future
and large, clean stature
nearer to all your nature.

. . . .

The latchpieces of consciousness unfasten.
We are stroked out of dream and night and myth,
and turning slowly to awareness, listen
to the soft bronchial whisperings of death.

Never forget in legendary darkness
the ways of the hands' turning and the mouth's ways,
wander in the fields of change and not remember
a voice and many voices and the evening's burning.

Turn and remember, this is the world made plain
by chart and signal, instrument and name :

to some we say Master, others call Sister,
to some we offer nothing but love :

flier in advance, the cloud over his mouth ;
the inventor who produces the moment of proof ;
a sun and moon and other several stars ;
and those who know each other over wars.

Cats stream upon a hill,
the poet-cock breaks his throat now to say :
Moment of Proof, May dawn transposing night,
partisan dawn's on the side of day!

      .   .   .   .   .

What hill can ever hold us?
                     Deeply night
found you intent upon this city river,
asleep at heart (turn light to her at last,
it shall be to her
as wellwater) :
going all day along the gilded air
you saw at midnight
(going, down to the river, haunted by fog-horns) :
steam escaping over the spouting manhole,
a rout of white cats racing through the street.
Wet street, and the fight was ended there,
cats and that cock, fearful antagonists
resolved in fog, a quick pack running uphill
to a cock rigid with joy; running, but not to kill.

      .   .   .   .   .

    "Forehead to forehead I meet thee, this third time,
                Moby Dick!"—Herman Melville

Moment of proof, when the body holds its vision.
masses recognize masses, knowledge without all end ;
face fathoms other face, all the hills open sunrise,
mouth sets on mouth ; Spring, and the tulips
               totter in the wind.

Forfeit in love, forfeit in conflict, here
met and at last marked clear in principle,

desire meets desire, the chase expands, and now
forever we course, knowing the marks of growth,
                    seeing the signals.

Now we remember winter-tormented cities,
the August farm's overgrown hollow, thick with goldenrod,
the impetus of strain, and places where
love set its terminals, the vivid hunger
                    and satisfying food.

Mayday is moment of proof, when recognition
binds us in protest, binds us under a sun
of love and subtle thought and the ductile wish.
Tomorrow's Mayday. — How many are we?
                    We'll be everyone.

No hill can ever hold us, peak enlists peak,
climax forces out climax, proud cock, cats streaming,
poets and pickets contriving a valid country,
: Mayday moment, forever provoking new
                    belief and blooming.

❧ II.
From U. S. 1 ❧

❧ GAULEY BRIDGE ❧

Camera at the crossing sees the city
a street of wooden walls and empty windows,
the doors shut handless in the empty street,
and the deserted Negro standing on the corner.

The little boy runs with his dog
up the street to the bridge over the river where
nine men are mending road for the government.
He blurs the camera-glass fixed on the street.

Railway tracks here and many panes of glass
tin under light, the grey shine of towns and forests:
in the commercial hotel (Switzerland of America)
the owner is keeping his books behind the public glass.

Postoffice window, a hive of private boxes,
the hand of the man who withdraws, the woman who reaches
    her hand
and the tall coughing man stamping an envelope.

The bus station and the great pale buses stopping for food;
April-glass-tinted, the yellow-aproned waitress;
coast-to-coast schedule on the plateglass window.

The man on the street and the camera eye:
he leaves the doctor's office, slammed door, doom,
any town looks like this one-street town.

Glass, wood, and naked eye : the movie-house
closed for the afternoon frames posters streaked with rain,
advertise "Racing Luck" and "Hitch-Hike Lady."

Whistling, the train comes from a long way away,
slow, and the Negro watches it grow in the grey air,
the hotel man makes a note behind his potted palm.

Eyes of the tourist house, red-and-white filling station,
the eyes of the Negro, looking down the track,
hotel-man and hotel, cafeteria, camera.

And in the beerplace on the other sidewalk
always one's harsh night eyes over the beerglass
follow the waitress and the yellow apron.

The road flows over the bridge,
Gamoca pointed at the underpass,
opposite, Alloy, after a block of town.

What do you want — a cliff over a city?
A foreland, sloped to sea and overgrown with roses?
These people live here.

ᮥ PRAISE OF THE COMMITTEE ᮥ

These are the lines on which a committee is formed.
   Almost as soon as work was begun in the tunnel
   men began to die among dry drills.   No masks.
   Most of them were not from the valley.
   The freights brought many every day from States
   all up and down the Atlantic seaboard
   and as far inland as Kentucky, Ohio.
   After the work the camps were closed or burned.
   The ambulance was going day and night,
   White's undertaking business thriving and
   his mother's cornfield put to a new use.
   "Many of the shareholders at this meeting
   "were nervous about the division of the profits;
   "how much has the Company spent on lawsuits?
   "The man said $150,000.   Special counsel:
   "I am familiar with the case.   Not : one : cent.

24 ᮥ

" 'Terms of the contract.   Master liable.'
"No reply.   Great corporation disowning men who
    made . . ."
After the lawsuits had been instituted . . .
The Committee is a true reflection of the will of the people.
Every man is ill.   The women are not affected,
This is not a contagious disease.   A medical commission,
Dr. Hughes, Dr. Hayhurst examined the chest
of Raymond Johnson, and Dr. Harless, a former
company doctor.   But he saw too many die,
he has written his letter to Washington.
The Committee meets regularly, wherever it can.
Here are Mrs. Jones, three lost sons, husband sick,
Mrs. Leek, cook for the bus cafeteria,
the men : George Robinson, leader and voice,
four other Negroes (three drills, one camp-boy)
Blankenship, the thin friendly man, Peyton the engineer,
Juanita absent, the one outsider member.
Here in the noise, loud belts of the shoe-repair shop,
meeting around the stove beneath the one bulb hanging.
They come late in the day.   Many come with them
who pack the hall, wait in the thorough dark.
This is a defense committee.   Unfinished business:
Two rounds of lawsuits, 200 cases
Now as to the crooked lawyers
If the men had worn masks, their use would have involved
time every hour to wash the sponge at mouth.
Tunnel, 3 miles long.   Much larger than
the Holland Tunnel or Pittsburgh's Liberty Tubes.
Total cost, say, $16,000,000.
This is the procedure of such a committee:
To consider the bill before the Senate.
To discuss relief.
    Active members may be cut off relief
        16-mile walk to Fayetteville for cheque—
    WEST VIRGINIA RELIEF ADMINISTRATION, #22991,
    TO JOE HENIGAN, GAULEY BRIDGE, ONE AND $^{50}/_{100}$,
    WINONA NATIONAL BANK.   PAID FROM STATE FUNDS.

25 ॐ

Unless the Defense Committee acts;
the *People's Press*, supporting this fight,
signed editorials, sent in funds.
Clothing for tunnel-workers.
  Rumored, that in the post-office
  parcels are intercepted.
  Suspected : Conley.   Sheriff, no hotelman,
  head of the town ring—
  Company whispers.   Spies,
  The Racket.
Resolved, resolved.
George Robinson holds all their strength together:
To fight the companies   to make somehow a future.
"At any rate, it is inadvisable to keep a community of dying
persons intact."
"Senator Holt.   Yes.   This is the most barbarous example
of industrial construction that ever happened in the world."
Please proceed.
"In a very general way Hippocrates' *Epidemics* speaks of the
    metal digger who breathes with difficulty, having a pain
    and wan complexion.
    Pliny, the elder. . . ."
"Present work of the Bureau of Mines. . . ."
The dam's pure crystal slants upon the river.
  A dark and noisy room, frozen two feet from stove.
  The cough of habit.   The sound of men in the hall
  waiting for word.

      These men breathe hard
      but the committee has a voice of steel.
      One climbs the hill on canes.
      They have broken the hills and cracked the riches wide.

      In this man's face
      family leans out from two worlds of graves—
      here is a room of eyes,
      a single force looks out, reading our life.

Who stands over the river?
Whose feet go running in these rigid hills?
Who comes, warning the night,
shouting and young to waken our eyes?

Who runs through electric wires?
Who speaks down every road?
Their hands touched mastery;   now they
demand an answer.

ঽ THE DISEASE ঽ

This is a lung disease. Silicate dust makes it.
The dust causing the growth of

This is the X-ray picture taken last April.
I would point out to you : these are the ribs;
this is the region of the breastbone;
this is the heart (a wide white shadow filled with blood).
In here of course is the swallowing tube, esophagus.
The windpipe. Spaces between the lungs.

                    Between the ribs?

Between the ribs. These are the collar bones.
Now, this lung's mottled, beginning, in these areas.
You'd say a snowstorm had struck the fellow's lungs.
About alike, that side and this side, top and bottom.
The first stage in this period in this case.

                    Let us have the second.

Come to the window again.   Here is the heart.
More numerous nodules, thicker, see, in the upper lobes.
You will notice the increase : here, streaked fibrous tissue—

Indicating?

That indicates the progress in ten months' time.
And now, this year — short breathing, solid scars
even over the ribs, thick on both sides.
Blood vessels shut.   Model conglomeration.

What stage?

Third stage.   Each time I place my pencil point:
There and there and there, there, there.

"It is growing worse every day.   At night
"I get up to catch my breath.   If I remained
"flat on my back I believe I would die."

It gradually chokes off the air cells in the lungs?
I am trying to say it the best I can.
That is what happens, isn't it?
A choking-off in the air cells?

Yes.
There is difficulty in breathing.
Yes.
And a painful cough?
Yes.

Does silicosis cause death?

Yes, sir.

• GEORGE ROBINSON : BLUES •

Gauley Bridge is a good town for Negroes, they let us stand
    around, they let us stand
around on the sidewalks if we're black or brown.
Vanetta's over the trestle, and that's our town.

The hill makes breathing slow, slow breathing after you
    row the river,
and the graveyard's on the hill, cold in the springtime blow,
the graveyard's up on high, and the town is down below.

Did you ever bury thirty-five men in a place in back of your
    house,
thirty-five tunnel workers the doctors didn't attend,
died in the tunnel camps, under rocks, everywhere, world
    without end.

When a man said I feel poorly, for any reason, any weakness
    or such,
letting up when he couldn't keep going barely,
the Cap and company come and run him off the job surely.

I've put them
DOWN from the tunnel camps
to the graveyard on the hill,
tin-cans all about — it fixed them!—

TUNNELITIS
hold themselves up
at the side of a tree,
I can go right now
to that cemetery.

When the blast went off the boss would call out, Come, let's
    go back,
when that heavy loaded blast went white, Come, let's go back,
telling us hurry, hurry, into the falling rocks and muck.

29 •

The water they would bring had dust in it, our drinking water,
the camps and their groves were colored with the dust,
we cleaned our clothes in the groves, but we always had the
    dust.

Looked like somebody sprinkled flour all over the parks and
    groves,
it stayed and the rain couldn't wash it away and it twinkled
that white dust really looked pretty down around our ankles.

As dark as I am, when I came out at morning after the tunnel
    at night,
with a white man, nobody could have told which man was white.
The dust had covered us both, and the dust was white.

❧ ALLOY ❧

This is the most audacious landscape. The gangster's
stance with his gun smoking and out is not so
vicious as this commercial field, its hill of glass.

Sloping as gracefully as thighs, the foothills
narrow to this, clouds over every town
finally indicate the stored destruction.

Crystalline hill: a blinded field of white
murdering snow, seamed by convergent tracks;
the travelling cranes reach for the silica.

And down the track, the overhead conveyor
slides on its cable to the feet of chimneys.
Smoke rises, not white enough, not so barbaric.

Here the severe flame speaks from the brick throat,
electric furnaces produce this precious, this clean,
annealing the crystals, fusing at last alloys.

Hottest for silicon, blast furnaces raise flames,
spill fire, spill steel, quench the new shape to freeze,
tempering it to perfected metal.

Forced through this crucible, a million men.
Above this pasture, the highway passes those
who curse the air, breathing their fear again.

The roaring flowers of the chimney-stacks
less poison, at their lips in fire, than this
dust that is blown from off the field of glass;

blows and will blow, rising over the mills,
crystallized and beyond the fierce corrosion
disintegrated angel on these hills.

❧ THE DAM ❧

All power is saved, having no end.   Rises
   in the green season, in the sudden season
   the white the budded
                    and the lost.
Water celebrates, yielding continually
sheeted and fast in its overfall
slips down the rock, evades the pillars
building its colonnades, repairs
in stream and standing wave
retains its seaward green
broken by obstacle rock; falling, the water sheet
spouts, and the mind dances, excess of white.
White brilliant function of the land's disease.

Many-spanned, lighted, the crest leans under
concrete arches and the channelled hills,
turns in the gorge toward its release;

kinetic and controlled, the sluice
urging the hollow, the thunder,
the major climax
                    energy
total and open watercourse
praising the spillway, fiery glaze,
crackle of light, cleanest velocity
flooding, the moulded force.

> *I open out a way over the water*
> *I form a path between the Combatants:*
> *Grant that I sail down like a living bird,*
> *power over the fields and Pool of Fire.*
> *Phoenix, I sail over the phoenix world.*

Diverted water, the fern and fuming white
ascend in mist of continuous diffusion.
Rivers are turning inside their mountains,
streams line the stone, rest at the overflow
lake and in lanes of pliant color lie.
Blessing of this innumerable silver,
printed in silver, images of stone
walk on a screen of falling water
in film-silver in continual change
recurring colored, plunging with the wave.

Constellations of light, abundance of many rivers.
The sheeted island-cities, the white surf filling west,
the hope, fast water spilled where still pools fed.
Great power flying deep: between the rock and the sunset,
the caretaker's house and the steep abutment,
hypnotic water fallen and the tunnels under
the moist and fragile galleries of stone,
mile-long, under the wave. Whether snow fall,
the quick light fall, years of white cities fall,
flood that this valley built falls slipping down
the green turn in the river's green.
Steep gorge, the wedge of crystal in the sky.

How many feet of whirlpools?
What is a year in terms of falling water?
Cylinders; kilowatts; capacities.
Continuity: $\Sigma Q = 0$
Equations for falling water. The streaming motion.
The balance-sheet of energy that flows
passing along its infinite barrier.

It breaks the hills, cracking the riches wide,
runs through electric wires;
it comes, warning the night,
running among these rigid hills,
a single force to waken our eyes.

They poured the concrete and the columns stood,
laid bare the bedrock, set the cells of steel,
a dam for monument was what they hammered home.
Blasted, and stocks went up;
insured the base,
and limousines
wrote their own graphs upon
roadbed and lifeline.

Their hands touched mastery:
wait for defense, solid across the world.
Mr. Griswold. "A corporation is a body without a soul."
Mr. Dunn. When they were caught at it they resorted to
     the methods employed by gunmen, ordinary machine-gun
     racketeers. They cowardly tried to buy out the people
     who had the information on them.
Mr. Marcantonio. I agree that a racket has been prac-
     tised, but the most damnable racketeering that I have
     ever known is the paying of a fee to the very attorney
     who represented these victims. That is the most outrag-
     eous racket that has ever come within my knowledge.
Miss Allen. Mr. Jesse J. Ricks, the president of the
     Union Carbide & Carbon Corporation, suggested that the

33 &

stockholder had better take this question up in a
private conference.
The dam is safe. A scene of power.
The dam is the father of the tunnel.
This is the valley's work, the white, the shining.

		Stock and Dividend in Dollars	Open	High	Low	Last	Net Chge.	----Closing----		
High	Low							Bid	Ask	Sales
111	61¼	Union Carbide (3.20)	67¼	69½	67¼	69½	+3	69¼	69½	3,400

The dam is used when the tunnel is used.
The men and the water are never idle,
have definitions.

This is a perfect fluid, having no age nor hours,
surviving scarless, unaltered, loving rest,
willing to run forever to find its peace
in equal seas in currents of still glass.
Effects of friction : to fight and pass again,
learning its power, conquering boundaries,
able to rise blind in revolts of tide,
broken and sacrificed to flow resumed.
Collecting eternally power. Spender of power,
torn, never can be killed, speeded in filaments,
million, its power can rest and rise forever,
wait and be flexible. Be born again.
Nothing is lost, even among the wars,
imperfect flow, confusion of force.
It will rise. These are the phases of its face.
It knows its seasons, the waiting, the sudden.
It changes. It does not die.

A FLASHING CLIFF

Spinning on his heel, the traveller
sees across snow a flashing cliff.
Past the plain's freeze, past savage branches
immune in ice, a frozen waterfall,
clamped in December, glistens alive.

Love, will you recognize yourself displayed?
Or is the age defective, cold as storm
to lock fast water in iron artifice,
whitening cataracts?—contempt and loss,
and nothing, in the great world, can lie calm,

travel alive, but is frozen solid,
and will not face its mirror nor speak its pain.
Will you fight winter to break in immense speed
resisting and sensitive, a waterfall-flash
sparkling full across the vicious plain?

Fight down our age, the mad vindictive time?
No victory's here. Now, any passion suffers
against proud ice, flashing, angry, and jailed.
You, maniac, catalept!
And, love. You are all rivers.

HOMAGE TO LITERATURE

When you imagine trumpet-faced musicians
blowing again inimitable jazz
no art can accuse nor cannonadings hurt,

or coming out of your dream of dirigibles
again see the unreasonable cripple
throwing his crutch headlong as the headlights

streak down the torn street, as the three hammerers
go One, Two, Three on the stake, triphammer poundings
and not a sign of new worlds to still the heart;

then stare into the lake of sunset as it runs
boiling, over the west past all control
rolling and swamps the heartbeat and repeats
sea beyond sea after unbearable suns;
think : poems fixed this landscape : Blake, Donne, Keats.

ಸ LOVER AS FOX ಸ

Driven, at midnight, to growth, the city's wistful turnings
lead you living on islands to some dark single house
where vacant windows mark increased pursuit,
chasing the runner outward beyond bounds
around the wildest circle of the night.

Circling returns! the city wreathed in rivers,
streaked skies surrounding islands of blank stone—
into this mythic track travelling breakneck,
a streaming furnace of escape, you, fox,
pursued, brick-red and vicious, circling bricks,

are followed as nimbly all mottled cloudy night;
fastened upon your path, the Floating Man
face down above the city, as shadow, changing shape,
as shadow of clouds, flying, and swiftly as
indifference running mad around the world.

Speed now! see city, houses across the water,
mosaic and bright over the riverfall
remote from the bursting eye, the open nostril,
flared lip (an image of angels singing speed),
caught in a nightlong visionary chase.

See the entire scene bright as you fly
round lots pauper all year, shacks lame with weather,
this sour fertile time teeming and ramshackle
before you, loving, clean sight in spyglass air.
And around town again. River, river.
Why do people live on islands?

ஃ THE DROWNING YOUNG MAN ஃ

The drowning young man lifted his face from the river
to me, exhausted from calling for help and weeping;
"My love!" I said; but he kissed me once for ever
and returned to his privacy and secret keeping.

His close face dripped with the attractive water,
I stared in his eyes and saw there penalty,
for the city moved in its struggle, loud about us,
and the salt air blew down; but he would face the sea.

"Afraid, afraid, my love?"   But he will never speak,
looking demands for rest, watching the wave come up,
too timid to turn, too loving to crying out,
lying face down in tide, biting his nervous lip.

Take him by shoulder and jaw, break his look back on us,
O hard to save, be saved, before we all shall drown!
But he has set his look, plunged his life deep for peace,
his face in the boiling river, and is surrendered down.

੬❖ BOY WITH HIS HAIR CUT SHORT ❖੭

Sunday shuts down on this twentieth-century evening.
The El passes. Twilight and bulb define
the brown room, the overstuffed plum sofa,
the boy, and the girl's thin hands above his head.
A neighbor radio sings stocks, news, serenade.

He sits at the table, head down, the young clear neck
        exposed,
watching the drugstore sign from the tail of his eye;
tattoo, neon, until the eye blears, while his
solicitous tall sister, simple in blue, bending
behind him, cuts his hair with her cheap shears.

The arrow's electric red always reaches its mark,
successful neon! He coughs, impressed by that precision.
His child's forehead, forever protected by his cap,
is bleached against the lamplight as he turns head
and steadies to let the snippets drop.

Erasing the failure of weeks with level fingers,
she sleeks the fine hair, combing: "You'll look fine tomorrow!
You'll surely find something, they can't keep turning you down;
the finest gentleman's not so trim as you!" Smiling, he raises
the adolescent forehead wrinkling ironic now.

He sees his decent suit laid out, new-pressed,
his carfare on the shelf. He lets his head fall, meeting
her earnest hopeless look, seeing the sharp blades splitting,
the darkened room, the impersonal sign, her motion,
the blue vein, bright on her temple, pitifully beating.

❧ NIGHT-MUSIC ❧

for Marya Zaturenska

TIME EXPOSURES

When the exposed spirit, busy in daytime,
searches out night, only renewer.
That time plants turn to. The world's table.
When any single thing's condemned again.
The changeable spirit finds itself out,
will not employ Saint Death, detective,
does its own hunting, runs at last to night.
Renewer, echo of judgment, morning-source, music.

Dark streets that light invents, one black tree standing,
struck by the street-light to raw electric green,
allow one man at a time to walk past, plain.
Cities lose size. The earth is field
and ranging these countries in sunset, we make quiet,
living in springtime, wish for nothing, see
glass bough, invented green, flower-sharp day
crackle into orange and be subdued to night.

The mind, propelled by work, reaches its evening:
slick streets, dog-tired, point the way to sleep,
walls rise in color, now summer shapes the Square
(and pastel five o'clock chalked on the sky).
We drive out to the suburbs, bizarre lawns
flicker a moment beside the speeding cars.
Speed haunts our ground, throws counties at us under
night, a black basin always spilling stars.

Waters trouble our quiet, vanishing down
reaches of hills whose image legend saves:
the foggy Venus hung above the flood
rising, rising, from the sea, with her arms full of waves
as ours are full of flowers.

Down polished airways a purple dove descending
sharp on the bodies of those so lately busy apart,
wingtip on breasttip, the deep body of feathers
in the breastgroove along the comforted heart.

The head inclined offers with love clear miles
of days simple in sun and action, bright
air poised about a face in ballet strictness
and pure pacific night.

But in our ears brute knocking at all doors,
factories bellow mutilation, and we live needly still
while strength and hours run
checkless downhill.

Flattered by grief, the changeable spirit
puts on importance. Goes into the street,
adventures everywhere but places fear
is absent. Everywhere the face's look
is absent, the heart is flat,
the avenues haunted by a head whose eye
runs tears incessantly, the other eye
narrow in smiling. Everywhere, words fail,
men sunk to dust, houses condemned, walls ruined,
and dust is never an anachronism.
Everywhere the eye runs tears. And here
the hand, propelled somehow, marches the room
pulling dark windowshades down around the gaze.

And now, stately, jotting on lipstick, she
prepares to sexualize her thistle thought.
Loosens her earrings, smiling. Drives
herself far into night. Smiles, fornicating. Drives
herself deep into sleep. Sees children sleep.

ADVENTURES, MIDNIGHT—II.

With those two I went driving in the dark,
out from our town in a borrowed car whose light
ate forests as we drove deeper into the park.

Beloved, spoke the sweet equivocal night—
those two stood clapped, each breast warmly on
    breast,
I stood apart to remove them from my sight:

The creased brook ran in continual unrest,
rising to seastorm in the rioting mind.
Here night and they and I—and who was merriest?

He turned his face away refusing, and so signed
for her to stop who too was comfortless
and equally needy, as tender and as blind.

On the road to the city stood the hedge whose
    darkness
had covered me months ago with that tall stranger
as foreign to me as this loneliness,

as enemy to me as tonight's anger
of grief in the country, shut with those two in
    the park:
this crying, frantic at removal, the dark, the
    sorrowful danger.

🐦 WOMAN AND EMBLEMS 🐦

WOMAN AND BIRD

A bird flew out of a cloud
(with a beak, flying),
broke its beak on my bone,
cried bird-cries over crying.

Sky, stranger, wilderness
(flying starry through flesh),
make an end; be me, bird.
It reverses my one wish.

Bird screams slavery among bones.
(I watch with a bird's eyes.)
Quarrel, wings; if I travel,
bird stays—stand, bird flies.

Bird sets feathers where flesh was
(my claws slide away on space).
Bird, here—now, bird, we fly!
Mourns, mourns, it turns a captive face.

THE BIRTHDAY

A sound lying on the fantastic air
opens the night and the child is born;
as the wind moves, the solemn crying
pioneers in the air, changes

to flame crusading among the grasses
fire-whitened, aroused before it,
rippled crops—and blazing races
into a central arena

where it stands as a fighting-cock
conqueror head, aggressive spur,

and the gilt feather, the bronze, the greenish,
flicker and threaten.

The feathers of the fighting-cock
become a tree, and casting seed,
raise potent forests at its side—
birth among burning.

The great magnetic branches sign
meaning on the record sky—
now rise, moon, stiffen, bird, and flames,
kill and engender.

Reversal, chameleon,
pursuing images—
recurrent birth offering other names,
a spool of brightness.

WOMAN AND MUSIC

This is a tall woman walking through a square
thinking what is a woman at midnight in a park
under bells, in the trivial and lovely hours
with images, violins, dancers approaching?

This is a woman sitting at a mirror
her back to the glass and all the dancers advancing,
or in a chair laughing at a bone
sitting upright in a chair
talking of ballet, flesh's impermanence.

This is a woman looking at a stage—
dancing—and all the parks, walks, hours
balanced against a tallest blue decor,
dancing—and all the parks, walks, hours
descend in brilliant water past the eyes
pursuing and forgotten and subdued
to blinding music, the deliberate strings.

ɛə III.
From A TURNING WIND ɛə

৩ READING TIME : 1 MINUTE 26 SECONDS ৩

The fear of poetry is the
fear : mystery and fury of a midnight street
of windows whose low voluptuous voice
issues, and after that there is no peace.

That round waiting moment in the
theatre : curtain rises, dies into the ceiling
and here is played the scene with the mother
bandaging a revealed son's head. The bandage is torn off.
Curtain goes down. And here is the moment of proof.

That climax when the brain acknowledges the world;
all values extended into the blood awake.
Moment of proof. And as they say Brancusi did,
building his bird to extend through soaring air,
as Kafka planned stories that draw to eternity
through time extended. And the climax strikes.

Love touches so, that months after the look of
blue stare of love, the footbeat on the heart
is translated into the pure cry of birds
following air-cries, or poems, the new scene.
Moment of proof. That strikes long after act.

They fear it. They turn away, hand up palm out
fending off moment of proof, the straight look, poem.
The prolonged wound-consciousness after the bullet's shot.
The prolonged love after the look is dead,
the yellow joy after the song of the sun.

❧ TARGET PRACTICE ❧

Near Mexico, near April, in the morning.
Desert where the sun casts his circles of power
on acquiescent sand shifting beneath them. Car
speeding among white landscapes;   suddenly
the permanent scene at the dead-center.

Photo, in circles of speed, how at raw barnside
father and son stand, man with his rifle up
levelled at heartpoint of a nailed-up bird
spread, wings against the wood. The boy's arm thrown
up over his eyes, flinching from coming shot.

Bullseye, you bullet! pinning down the scene.
And speed you car over the waste of noon
into the boundaries of distance where
the first ring lessens into memory.
Until, a little lower than the sun,

centered in that last circle, hangs a free
fierce bird down-staring on the target of land,
circle on circle of power spread, and speeding
eyes passing from zone to zone, from war to where
their bullets will never bring him down.

❧ NUNS IN THE WIND ❧

As I came out of the New York Public Library
you said your influence on my style would be noticed
and from now on there would be happy poems.
                    It was at that moment
the street was assaulted by a covey of nuns
going directly toward the physics textbooks.

Tragic fiascos shadowed that whole spring.
The children sang streetfuls, and I thought:
O to be the King in the carol
kissed and at peace;   but recalling Costa Brava
the little blossoms in the mimosa tree
and later, the orange cliff, after they sent me out,
I knew there was no peace.

        You smiled, saying : Take it easy.

That was the year of the five-day fall of cities.
       First day, no writers. Second, no telephones. Third
       no venereal diseases. Fourth, no income tax. And on
       the fifth, at noon.
The nuns blocked the intersections, reading.
I used to go walking in the triangle of park,
seeing that locked face, the coarse enemy skin,
the eyes with all the virtues of a good child,
but no child was there, even when I thought, Child!
The 4 a.m. cop could never understand.
You said, not smiling, You are the future for me,
but you were the present and immediate moment
and I am empty-armed without, until to me is given
two lights to carry : my life and the light of my death.

If the wind would rise, those black throbbing umbrellas
fly downstreet, the flapping robes unfolding,
my dream would be over, poisons cannot linger
when the wind rises. . . .

All that year, the classical declaration of war was lacking.
There was a lot of lechery and disorder.
And I am queen on that island.

Well, I said suddenly in the tall and abstract room,
time to wake up.
Now make believe you can help yourself alone.
And there it was, the busy crosstown noontime
crossing, peopled with nuns.

Now, bragging now,
the flatfoot slambang victory,
                    thanks to a trick of wind
will you see faces blow, and though their bodies
by God's grace will never blow,
cities shake in the wind, the year's over,
calendars tear, and their clothes blow. O yes!

&ᴥ DEMOCRITUS LAUGHED &ᴥ

Democritus laughed when he
saw his whole universe
combined of atoms, and
the gods destroyed —
He killed the ghostly
vengeance deep at the source,
holding bright philosophical sand
up for a threat —
laughing his soldier laughter
with ages of troops after
who grin with reason in
the trenches of
metaphysics, astronomy, disease,
philosophy, the state, and poetry,
the black-and-white war on sin,
the dead wars, the impossible dark wars,
the war on starve, the war on kill, the war on love,
the war on peace.

CORRESPONDENCES

Wars between wars, laughter behind the lines.
Fighting behind the lines. Not children laughing,
but the trench-laughter of the wounded, of radios,
of animal cartoons, the lonely broadcast
on the taxi dashboard, behind the wrecking crew
lit by a naked bulb — to the forgetful bars
prisms and amber shaken with laughter, to the ships at sea.
To the maleficent walls of cities, and an old actress
trying against the trying wind under the skyscrapers,
blind ageing face up, still the look of the lioness,
walking close to the buildings, along the wall,
she licks her lips in panic of loneliness.
She understands the laughter that rides around the streets,
blowing the news to the stone-lands, the swamp-lands, the
     dust-land,
where omens of war, restless in clouds of dust,
mean dust is never an anachronism
and ruin's news.

The actress knows. Laughter takes up the slack,
changes the fact, narrowing it to nothing,
hardly a thing but silence on a stage.
Crack of laughter. Walls go white, and the plain open note
talks in a houseful of noise. Reply : Now hide!

Over the air, the blindfold answer, the news of force,
the male and hairless hand of fear
in a shiny leather sleeve
armed.

The radiations of harm : black grooves in photographs,
blackness in spokes playing from Hitler's head.
A head with one nightmare.
Expect failure of plans, the floodgates closing,
failure of traffic-control, loss of voice, fog.

Wires dead, defection of your central power-plant.
A code : Laughter. What alphabet are they using?

Many wished for little.
Many asked unity.

We had our characters as we had our cities,
or as a lyric poet has his voices, audible
as separate lives, maturing in poise, and symbols
coming to their "great period," too big to kill,
able to batter at the jetties of hell.

Rites of initiation of our lives:
by filth in childhood,
by wealth in the middle,
by death at the end.
We knew the dear, the enemy, we saw the spy
whisper at ear, the agency suggest,
and where no secrecy and treason were
we saw the novelist, pimp of character,
develop the age so it be understood
to read like his book, a city of the dead.

But the century had its rites, its politics,
machineries whose characters were wars.
Ceremonies of further separation. And now, our backs to brick,
war closes in, calling us to the guns
to make accounting how our time was spent.
And the planes fall. Soon the whole incident is
over, all but the consequences.

Laughter, and childhood; and laughter; and age; or death.
Call to the male puppet, Croak,
and to the female puppet, Shriek,
and turn on me your gun for luck.

Take us our sacrifices, a wish for the living,
this foil of thought, this soil from which we sprang,

fugal music of peace, the promises well-kept,
the big and little diaries of the dead.
The song of occupations and the ghosts,
the historian, pimp of centuries, the general, pimp of wars,
the Floating Man, gentle above the cities,
afraid to touch, a cloud before his head,
laughing the laugh of a man about to be drafted,
the flier, mock-protagonist of his time,
refugees who reserve a final condemnation
and see a richer horror in the sky.

Humor, saliva of terror, will not save the day
or even one moment when the cities are
high in a boneyard where clowns ride up and down
and a night crew works quickly before morning;
while news arrives of the death of others,
laughter of brothers and the brother wars,
works of an age among such characters.

Violent electric night! and the age spiralling past
and the sky turning over, and the wind turning the stars.

GIBBS

It was much later in his life he rose
in the professors' room, the frail bones rising
among that fume of mathematical meaning,
symbols, the language of symbols, literature . . . threw
air, simple life, in the dead lungs of their meeting,
said, "Mathematics *is* a language."

Withdrew. Into a silent world beyond New Haven,
the street-fights gone, the long youth of undergraduate
riots down Church Street, initiation violence,

secret societies gone : a broken-glass isolation,
bottles smashed flat, windows out, street-fronts broken:

to quiet,
the little portico, wrought-iron and shutters' house.
A usable town, a usable tradition.

In war or politics.
Not science.

Withdrew.

Civil War generates, but
Not here. Tutors Latin after his doctorate
when all of Yale is disappearing south.

There is no disorganization, for there is no passion.
Condense, he is thinking.   Concentrate, restrict.
This is the state permits the whole to stand,
the whole which is simpler than any of its parts.
And the mortars fired, the tent-lines, lines of trains,
earthworks, breastworks of war, field-hospitals,
Whitman forever saying, "Identify."
Gibbs saying
"I wish to know systems.

To be in this work.   Prepare an apocryphal
cool life in which nothing is not discovery
and all is given, levelly, after clearest
most disciplined research.

The German years
of voyage, calmer than Kant in Koenigsberg, to states
where laws are passed and truth's a daylight gift.

Return to a house inheriting Julia's keys,
sister receiving all the gifts of the world,
white papers on your desk.

Spiritual gift
she never took.

Books of discovery,
haunted by steam, ghost of the disembodied engine,
industrialists in their imperious designs

made flower an age to be driven far by this
serene impartial acumen.
                            Driving
his sister's coach in the city, knowing the
rose of direction loosing its petals down
atoms and galaxies.   Diffusion's absolute.
Phases of matter!   The shouldering horses pass
turnings (snow, water, steam) echoing platted curves,
statues of diagrams, the forms of schemes
to stand white on a table, real as phase,
or as the mountainous summer curves when he
under New Hampshire lay while shouldering night
came down upon him then with all its stars.
Gearing that power-spire to the wide air.
Exacting symbols of rediscovered worlds.

Through evening New Haven drove. The yellow window
of Sloane Lab all night shone.

Shining an image whole, as a streak of brightness
bland on the quartz, light-blade on Iceland spar
doubled! and the refraction carrying fresh clews.
Withdrew.
                    It will be an age of experiment,
or mysticism, anyway vastest assumption.
He makes no experiments.   Impregnable retires.
Anyone having these desires will make these researches.
Laws are the gifts of their systems, and the man
in constant tension of experience drives
moments of coexistence into light.
It is the constitution of matter I must touch.

Deduction from deduction : entropy,
heat flowing down a gradient of nature,
perpetual glacier driving down the side
of the known world in an equilibrium tending
to uniformity, the single dream.

                                        He binds
himself to know the public life of systems.
Look through the wounds of law
at the composite face of the world.

                    If Scott had known,
he would not die at the Pole, he would have been
saved, and again saved — here, gifts from overseas,
and grapes in January past Faustus' grasp.
Austerity, continence, veracity, the full truth flowing
not out from the beginning and the base,
but from accords of components whose end is truth.
Thought resting on these laws enough becomes
an image of the world, restraint among
breaks manacles, breaks the known life before
Gibbs' pale and steady eyes.

                                    He knew the composite
many-dimensioned spirit, the phases of its face,
found the tremendous level of the world,
Energy : Constant, but entropy, the spending,
tends toward a maximum — a "mixed-up-ness,"
and in this end of levels to which we drive
in isolation, to which all systems tend,
Withdraw, he said clearly.

The soul says to the self : I will withdraw,
the self saying to the soul : I will withdraw,
and soon they are asleep together
spiralling through one dream.

                                    Withdrew, but in
his eager imperfect timidities, rose and dared
sever waterspouts, bring the great changing world
time makes more random, into its unity.

RYDER

Call himself unbegun, for the sea made him;   assemblage of
        waters gave him his color.
But not the sea;   coast-line, coast-water, rising sfumato from
        smoke-holes of the sea,
pitching onto the black rock of the ocean-edge.   But not the
        coast-line;
the Atlantic coast, flinging him headlong from its rigors into his
        art.
Great salt-swept boldface captain, big-boned New Englander
        drowning deep
among the mysteries of the painful western adventure, circling
in unappeased circles into America.

Tempests, phantasmagoria!   Impervious, first of all
to paint the tragic landscape that breeds us here,
the deep life, the terrible foreboding whose soil
is in our mind, the imagination of this geography.
Whose whaling port acknowledges the fearful
content of evil and the swift-lit blessed light,
Melville's 'latent horror of life' in the whale water
that Ryder, whose racecourse with its big horse Death
runs round the brain, knew.
                              In his room
wreckage of boxes, propped-leg, easel, couch, ashes, coal-keg, shells,
bronzed tarnished coffee-pot, books, paints, piled broken furniture,
varnish drippings, matches, cans, newspapers stacked up,
plaster falling with a scurrying like mice, paper bannering from the
        walls,
the stains, the path cleared to the stuffed chair crammed with
        poems,
money, checks, poems, the bathtub filled with clothes—
the unseen room, after a moment there.
He stood
                laying the paint on
                              stacking color on,

more pigment, dark and stormy, thickness, depth, more black,
    stove-ashes maybe,
and at the last slashed poker through the cloth, a knife of lightning,
    white as space, leaping white! out of darkness!
Out black night leaping, rider to flame.

He walks through the rainy streets, the great grey sweater;
fog walking through rain, wool worn on his giant head,
his giant beard stowed in the collar.   Walks black pavement.
Is seen on corners beaten by storms of night.
He gives a painting to the tubercular seamstress
"to look at while she lives," talks poetry
and philosophy to the woman at the newsstand.
He believes with his eye, he lives in the foreboding
empty tempests of the mind, thunder revolving
among his blackest noons;   remembers voyages
to fabulous harbors whose event was sea.

He looks through the plateglass window at his formal dinner,
turns down the street, "I have been there," looks through glass
at formal painting, inch by inch, reaching the corner
stands back, "That's a fine place."   And moves away
to mystic reconciliations, feeling the world enlarge
and never complete itself, a bone riding a horse
around a track, dead angels from the sea resurrected
to lend a metaphor of waves, to sound the abstract
Jonah who rolls under a pitch of ocean,
knows God with his arms up among the teeth of waves,
the moon stark in the sky as a center of whirlpool.
All these invoke the image, a sea-belief in the sea
whose waters open swallow the army whole and save the tribe.

He is your irresponsible pioneer. He is deprived. Fearful of sex.
        Desire, God's blossoming rod
points to assemblages of waters, heroes Macbeth kneedeep,
the foggy Dutchman riding, salt eyelids see
the fall of waters, the distinction and power, the shock,
the helplessness immanent in things.

Ghosts of oxen, stiff-grappled claws of a dead bird,
romantic wish that mourns from an Opera seat
over the spotlit love, wishes housekeeper love,
Elaine of wish, bends over an empty big suit of armor,
over the giant fallen bones of the dead horse.

Historic disherison : Ryder, emblematist,
divorced from the arts, believing in art alone,
master of meaning and never mastering means,
wasteful and slow, without tradition.   He shortens
the life of his paintings in their friable colors
by ignorance, by storms.   Refusing the dead life
like a nest of tables whose next is always smaller
refined and congruent, slashes American sky
by derelict lightning, turning all landscape into
sublunar ocean.   He is chained under water,
chained under rain, under paint, no hold on daylight,
his fixed moon stares into a tragic coast
whose people are little figures pasted on.
"Not you," he cries, "the human document."
These are not paintings for comfort hung on walls.
Paint over it, paint.   It is a monument
cracking and supernatural, an obelisk at the sea,
three sides shadowed with names, the sea-slab empty.
A big-boned charging figure under rain
seen by the visionary moon and dark,
unbegun among assemblages of waves.
His head that was moon the center of the storm.
His boulders that were eyes washed by the drift of ocean.

❧ CHAPMAN ❧

Returns to punishment as we all return, in agonized initiation
    proving America,
a country returning to moments of conversion, in agony supporting
    its changes, receiving
the past, the clews of instinct, and the rich return:
conviction in our people's face, all in pain.
He dances in Boston, the young and turning side
turned to a room of marvellous skirts whose rustle
like burning paper alters, rustling black to flame.
He looks across all rooms to a sibyl-minded woman
the dark   the clew to life   whose afternoons
he shares through Dante's climbing Paradise
to break his youth, the handsome turning side
dancing and turning again to her dark head
in rings of darkness whose God is ringed in light
which coils and revolves around him—
in the smoky garden
after the word was spoken
the blow to the rival's smoky head echoing in the hand
ringed round with darkness;
dark passages through streets unknown; and now, at home,
he sees his braced arm, ringing with the shock,
given before him to the ringing fire.

Blaze of hard-coal.   Disapparition of flesh.
He draws his hand out of flame; charred to the bone,
white knuckles and finger-bones exposed.
His soul rises screaming in the shape of an eagle.
He says, quietly and exactly, "This will never do."
"The one time in my life I lived was twenty days of pain."
And later, after the healing, after the marriage,
alone among red desert, the wild bushes' grey-green,
the red buttes cancelling half the sky, he writes
"It was not waste land in Colorado.   Not waste time, for
"you are here and many lives packed into one life,

"the green shoot out of the heart of the plant, springing up
      blossoms in the night;
"many old things have put on immortality,
"and lost things have come back knocking within
"from before the time I was conceived in the womb,
"there were you also.
"And of the pain! it was false,
"and the rending, unnecessary.
"The breaking down of dams that ought never be up,
"but being up it was the sweeping away
"that the waters might flow together."

The life all burning on the public hill,
the men living tramort, travelling through their deaths,
arrive with marks by which they know one another
at the center of systems.   By a breach of childhood
symptoms of health declare all the signs leading through,
until the crisis comes,
air seethes, and all the bushes flicker up,
memories parasite in the life underground
irrupt with convulsions and the speech of fire.

At the focus, the cool life is insufficient.
He knows his conversion.   He speaks of Whitman as tramp:
"By an act as simple as death, he puts off effort and lives in peace."
Knowing by what redemption he claims his house,
he stands on the balcony of a burning building.
The ghosts come near the blood.   Sits at the bedside reading
to the dropped quiet head, Dante and fire and coexistent death
at his wife's bedside.
Fire, rage, splendor;   and terror
who judges the judgment of men.
He is broken, his face is broken back,
his spirit's legs are broken, crutches hold him,
a second wife holds him while he becomes
incredible to himself, fulgurite fused by lightning,
health shaking its flag of death in his frenetic head.

61 ॐ

Death of his son, and he heals, he is born again,
fed on his agonies, wanting again
his gritty taste of truth.

There are those who are many-born.   There is the man
who will plunge his hand in the fire this evening, who goes out
        every day
seeing Prometheus in mirrors, finding
comets, men of the people, conscious, who take their place
in national revulsion producing a nation's poems,
belong to the present, are not sterilized
by breaks from the past.
He fights for the acute senses, terror, passion, and need.
"I make it a policy to say nothing I will not regret."
Speaks from a cart-end, manhandles his hecklers,
knows the struggles of treason making it easy for death
to arrive when the living have passed the perfection of youth.

The century bursts upward in shocks of flame,
fireworks' starfish of imperial spirit,
ordeals by fire : he fights the finished wars,
looks back to slavery.   They burn the shingles down,
the lynched face broken back, mouth filled with fire,
firebrand full in face.   The ashes rise.
Chapman arrives to face his empty hall,
courtly, one-handed, turning his handsome side
upon the hall to face his audience,
one Negro woman come to hear.   Undoings
walking in all forms, treacheries of the deep
spirit caught in the net.   Our need is of new life.
There are these tendencies in America:
they planned John Brown;   they do what will be done.

Birth after birth, in the spanned democratic
passage of birth, the incubation motive,
desire's experience, tense for finality.
He is reborn too often;   the shock cannot take.
He loosens;   fights for war;   fights Harvard's plans:

a stone for both sides — he rants, upholstered deep
in Harvard Club armchairs — a monument to Zero.
He is charred out, is calling vengeance on Jews,
he is old and charred.   He has been many-born.
Blinks in the fire-world, sees started birds
blinked red and black, the wing a dark log burning
against the sun;   flashes of cypress and swamps,
a watery forest of red birds.
Goes down
his altering ash smothers the shock of peace,
he carries flame
but selling-out is not a dramatic moment,
is the chain of memories parasite,
the thin flame of existence travelling down
until the yellow and alizarin red
flares out.   The whole of any life, he said,
is always unmistakably one thing.
And a dream-voice said Freiheit
a crackling globe flew down
fire and punishment, returning grace;
vortex of parable through modes of life
simple and imperceptible transitions
in countries of transition giving other lives
the long remorseless logic of their love.

❧ ANN BURLAK ❧

Let her be seen, a voice on a platform, heard
as a city is heard in its prophetic sleep when
one shadow hangs over one side of a total wall
of houses, factories, stacks, and on the faces
around her tallies, shadow from one form.

An open square shields the voice, reflecting it
to faces who receive its reflections of light as

change on their features. She stands alone, sending
her voice out to the edges, seeing approach people
to make the ring ragged, to fill in blacker
answers.
      This is an open square of the lit world
whose dark sky over hills rimmed white with evening
squares lofts where sunset lies in dirty patterns
and rivers of mill-towns beating their broken bridges
as under another country full of air.
Dark offices evening reaches where letters take the light
even from palest faces over script.
Many abandon machines, shut off the looms,
hurry on glooming cobbles to the square. And many
are absent, as in the sky about her face, the birds
retreat from charcoal rivers and fly far.

The words cluster about the superstition mountains.
The sky breaks back over the torn and timid
her early city whose stacks along the river
flourished darkness over all, whose mottled sky
shielded the faces of those asleep in doorways
spread dark on narrow fields through which the father
comes home without meat, the forest in the ground
whose trees are coal, the lurching roads of autumn
where the flesh of the eager hangs, heavier by
its thirty bullets, barbed on wire. Truckdrivers
swing ungrazed trailers past, the woman in the fog
can never speak her poems of unemployment,
the brakeman slows the last freight round the curve.
And riveters in their hardshell fling short fiery
steel, and the servant groans in his narrow room,
and the girl limps away from the door of the shady doctor.
Or the child new-born into a company town
whose life can be seen at birth as child, woman, widow.
The neighbor called in to nurse the baby of a spy,
the schoolboy washing off the painted word
"scab" on the front stoop, his mother watering flowers
pouring the milk-bottle of water from the ledge,

who stops in horror, seeing. The grandmother going
down to her cellar with a full clothes-basket,
turns at the shot, sees men running past brick,
smoke-spurt and fallen face.
                              She speaks of these:
the chase down through the canal, the filling-station,
stones through the windshield. The woman in the bank
who topples, the premature birth brought on by tear-gas,
the charge leaving its gun slow-motion, finding those
who sit at windows knowing what they see;
who look up at the door, the brutalized face appraising
strangers with holsters;   little blackened boys
with their animal grins, quick hands salvaging coal
among the slag of patriotic hills.

She knows the field of faces at her feet,
remembrances of childhood, likenesses of parents,
a system of looms in constellation whirled,
disasters dancing.
                    And behind her head
the world of the unpossessed, steel mills in snow flaming,
nine o'clock towns whose deputies' overnight power
hurls waste into killed eyes, whose guns predict
mirages of order, an empty coat before the blind.
Doorways within which nobody is at home.
The spies who wait for the spy at the deserted crossing,
a little dead since they are going to kill.
Those women who stitch their lives to their machines
and daughters at the symmetry of looms.

She speaks to the ten greatest American women:
The anonymous farmer's wife, the anonymous clubbed picket,
the anonymous Negro woman who held off the guns,
the anonymous prisoner, anonymous cotton-picker
trailing her robe of sack in a proud train,
anonymous writer of these and mill-hand, anonymous city-walker,
anonymous organizer, anonymous binder of the illegally wounded,
anonymous feeder and speaker to anonymous squares.

She knows their faces, their impatient songs
of passionate grief risen, the desperate music
poverty makes, she knows women cut down
by poverty, by stupid obscure days,
their moments over the dishes, speaks them now,
wrecks with the whole necessity of the past
behind the debris, behind the ordinary
smell of coffee, the ravelling clean wash,
the turning to bed, undone among savage night
planning and unplanning seasons of happiness
broken in dreams or in the jaundiced morning
over a tub or over a loom or over
the tired face of death.
                         She knows
the songs : *Hope to die, Mo I try, I comes out,*
Owin boss mo, I comes out, Lawd, Owin boss mo
food, money and life.
                      Praise breakers,
praise the unpraised who cannot speak their name.
Their asking what they need as unbelieved
as a statue talking to a skeleton.
They are the animals who devour their mother
from need, and they know in their bodies other places,
their minds are cities whose avenues are named
each after a foreign city. They fall when cities fall.
They have the cruelty and sympathy of those
whose texture is the stress of existence woven
into revenge, the crime we all must claim.
They hold the old world in their new world's arms.
And they are the victims, all the splinters of war
run through their eyes, their black escaping face
and runaway eyes are the Negro in the subway
whose shadowy detective brings his stick
down on the naked head as the express pulls in,
swinging in locomotive roars on skull.
They are the question to the ambassador
long-jawed and grim, they stand on marble, waiting
to ask how the terms of the strike have affected him.

66 ॐ

Answer : "I've never seen snow before. It's marvellous."
They stand with Ann Burlak in the rotunda, knowing
her insistent promise of life, remembering
the letter of the tear-gas salesman : "I hope
"this strike develops and a damn bad one too.
"We need the money."
                              This is the boundary
behind a speaker : Main Street and railroad tracks,
post office, furniture store. The soft moment before storm.
Since there are many years.
And the first years were the years of need,
the bleeding, the dragged foot, the wilderness,
and the second years were the years of bread
fat cow, square house, favorite work,
and the third years are the years of death.
The glittering eye all golden. Full of tears.
Years when the enemy is in our street,
and liberty, safe in the people's hands,
is never safe and peace is never safe.

Insults of attack arrive, insults
of mutilation. She knows the prophetic past,
many have marched behind her, and she knows
Rosa whose face drifts in the black canal,
the superstitions of a tragic winter
when children, their heads together, put on tears.
The tears fall at their throats, their chains are made
of tears, and as bullets melted and as bombs let down
upon the ominous cities where she stands
fluid and conscious. Suddenly perceives
the world will never daily prove her words,
but her words live, they issue from this life.
She scatters clews. She speaks from all these faces
and from the center of a system of lives
who speak the desire of worlds moving unmade
saying, "Who owns the world?" and waiting for the cry.

IVES

Knowing the voices of the country, gathering
voices of other harvest, farm-hands who gather in
sources of music on the blueberry hills,
the village band, lines at the schoolhouse singing—
lit cheeks and lips over the blown-glass lamps
in the broad houses, along the pebble beach,
or up the baldface mountain's granite sky
above New England, voices of wilderness,
scorch of the sun where ranges all run west,
snow-glare on seaward slopes, sea-breeze and tea,
the voices of stinted music in the towns.
There are strange herbs in the pasture, and the stiff
death angels on the red assyrian stones.
Daguerreotypes and family quiet, wells,
woodwork and panelling, the cloaks of the forest,
all the blinds drawn on the imagination's
immediate mystery of the passer-by.
Intense as instruments to split these sounds
into component memory, and reduce
memory to uncompromising sound.

To whom do I speak today?   I've heard their oarlocks turning
at dawn on the river, in the warm bankside light
heard cut trees fall, hickory pull the head
toward violent foreground laughter of torn wood,
watched steeples diminishing in low day before sunset,
and found the evening train riding the bend.
That train will never speak again of tracks
routed to outland counties, but the firm
sumac and corn, broadleaf tobacco farms,
a churchyard murmur for the air of truth,
acres where birds I did not know till now
fly sharp-reflected in water, a field of sky;
over the human lake, the gods make the swallows fly.

To whom do I speak today?   Call off your wit and write
for silent implicated men, a crabbed line

of intercepted music with the world between.
Networks of songs, white seagull in white air,
cliff edge and stripe of sand's immovable gulls
hung over women's morning festivals.
Affection of villages whose boy guitarist,
blond, with his rolled sleeve and the girl behind
sings into fire-darkness goodbye after pleasure
and the streets, our liberty, the village store,
songs of the sorrow and mystery of pavilions'
slow carousel-music, bulbs and mirrors in sunlight,
processions of godly animals revolving;
or big October mornings, cider and perry noon
when the child comes open-mouth round the corner singing;
that music of the imagination here
which is the only sound lives after war.

Acoustics of sideshows! and the organist
playing the mirror of the mind again.
Concord whose choice between repose and truth
colors our memory, whose outer islands of thought
are fugal movements in one dignity.
Rebellion of outposts whose deepest results arrive
when the rebellion, not from worst to greatest,
but great to greater goes.   The sequent movements
of that developing know supernatural
Hawthorne as dripping wet with guilt, a ghost
personal at first, and national at twilight,
and tries to be universal suddenly at midnight;
know in their pace the supernatural future
and the future of human coarseness, and Emerson's
future, eternity, whose forecast is the past,
and Alcott's suffering, whipping his innocent
boy next to the guilty, since guilt need not suffer;
and Thoreau who did not die of his consumption
but lived with it.
                    Raise us an instrument
limitless, without the scarecrow keyboard
can give repose and fame to successful pianists
playing to camouflage dullness.   A scale for truth,

obscurities of a village organist
who satisfies his life on Sunday.

Songs.
Young men singing on stoops, the sickle pears of Concord,
the wheels scraping the curb, lockets of childhood
faith, barn dances, ballads;   or those revealing men
I gave a mask, and they to me the secrets
of sensual thought, music and thunderbolt.
The concentrated man bent over drums,
a skeleton over drums, a fritter of triangles
played without aim, spasms of arabesques
in decoration of nothing.   I speak a flute over frost,
hypnotisms of trumpets, the plain and open voice
of the walk toward the future, commonplace transcendent
chores and melodeons, band-concert morning
or the ultimate Negro over his white piano
meaning O Saint!   O Blues!

This is Charles Ives.
Gold-lettered insurance windows frame his day.
He is eclectic, he sorts tunes like potatoes
for better next-year crops, catching the variable
wildest improvisations, his clusters of meaning;
railing against the fake sonorities, "sadness
"of a bathtub when the water is being let out,"
knowing the local hope knocking in any blood.
"Today we do not choose To die or to dance,
"but to live and walk."

Inventor, beginner of strong
coherent substance of music, knowing all
apple-reflecting streams, loons across echoing lake,
cities and men, as liners aloof in voyage,
and their dead eyes, so much blue in the ground
as water, as running song he loves and pours
as water into water, music in music.

Walks
at starfall or under the yellow dragons of sunset

70 છ๖

among the ritual answers and the secular wish,
among spruce, and maroon of fallen needles, walks
the pauper light of dawn imagining truth,
turning from recommended madness, from Europe
who must be forced to eat what she kills, from cities
where all the throats are playing the same tune
mechanically.

        He was young.   He did not climb
four flights on hands and knees to the piano.   Heard
the band in the square, Jerusalem the Golden
from all the rooftops, blare of foreground horns,
violins past the common;   in the street
the oral dissonance, the drum's array.
Far breaking music indistinct with wheels'
irregular talk, the moving world, the real
personal disagreement of many voices;
clusters of meaning break in fantastic flame,
silver of instruments rising behind the eye.

He gathers the known world total into music,
passion of sense, perspective's mask of light
into suggestion's inarticulate
gesture, invention.   Knowing the voices, knowing
these faces and music and this breeding landscape
balanced between the crisis and the cold
which bears the many-born, he parcels silence
into a music which submerges prayer,
rising as rivers of faces overhead,
naming the instruments we all must hold.

⃦ IV.
From BEAST IN VIEW ⃦

AJANTA

I—THE JOURNEY

Came in my full youth to the midnight cave
Nerves ringing; and this thing I did alone.
Wanting my fulness and not a field of war,
For the world considered annihilation, a star
Called Wormwood rose and flickered, shattering
Bent light over the dead boiling up in the ground,
The biting yellow of their corrupted lives
Streaming to war, denying all our words.
Nothing was left among the tainted weather
But world-walking and shadowless Ajanta.
Hallucination and the metal laugh
In clouds, and the mountain-spectre riding storm.
Nothing was certain but a moment of peace,
A hollow behind the unbreakable waterfall.
All the way to the cave, the teeming forms of death,
And death, the price of the body, cheap as air.
I blessed my heart on the expiation journey
For it had never been unable to suffer:
When I met the man whose face looked like the future,
When I met the whore with the dying red hair,
The child myself who is my murderer.
So came I between heaven and my grave
Past the serene smile of the *voyeur*, to
This cave where the myth enters the heart again.

II—THE CAVE

Space to the mind, the painted cave of dream.
This is not a womb, nothing but good emerges:
This is a stage, neither unreal nor real,
Where the walls are the world, the rocks and palaces
Stand on a borderland of blossoming ground.
If you stretch your hand, you touch the slope of the world
Reaching in interlaced gods, animals, and men.

There is no background.   The figures hold their peace
In a web of movement.   There is no frustration,
Every gesture is taken, everything yields connections.
The heavy sensual shoulders, the thighs, the blood-born flesh
And earth turning into color, rocks into their crystals,
Water to sound, fire to form; life flickers
Uncounted into the supple arms of love.
The space of these walls is the body's living space;
Tear open your ribs and breathe the color of time
Where nothing leads away, the world comes forward
In flaming sequences.   Pillars and prisms.   Riders
And horses and the figures of consciousness,
Red cow grows long, goes running through the world.
Flung into movement in carnal purity,
These bodies are sealed—warm lip and crystal hand
In a jungle of light.   Color-sheeted, seductive
Foreboding eyelid lowered on the long eye,
Fluid and vulnerable.   The spaces of the body
Are suddenly limitless, and riding flesh
Shapes constellations over the golden breast,
Confusion of scents and illuminated touch—
Monster touch, the throat printed with brightness,
Wide outlined gesture where the bodies ride.
Bells, and the spirit flashing.   The religious bells,
Bronze under the sunlight like breasts ringing,
Bronze in the closed air, the memory of walls,
Great sensual shoulders in the web of time.

III—LES TENDRESSES BESTIALES

A procession of caresses alters the ancient sky
Until new constellations are the body shining:
There's the Hand to steer by, there the horizon Breast,
And the Great Stars kindling the fluid hill.
All the rooms open into magical boxes,
Nothing is tilted, everything flickers
Sexual and exquisite.
The panther with its throat along my arm

Turns black and flows away.
Deep in all streets passes a faceless whore
And the checkered men are whispering one word.
The face I know becomes the night-black rose.
The sharp face is now an electric fan
And says one word to me.
The dice and the alcohol and the destruction
Have drunk themselves and cast.
Broken bottle of loss, and the glass
Turned bloody into the face.
Now the scene comes forward, very clear.
Dream-singing, airborne, surrenders the recalled,
The gesture arrives riding over the breast,
Singing, singing, tender atrocity,
The silver derelict wearing fur and claws.
O love, I stood under the apple branch,
I saw the whipped bay and the small dark islands,
And night sailing the river and the foghorn's word.
My life said to you : I want to love you well.
The wheel goes back and I shall live again,
But the wave turns, my birth arrives and spills
Over my breast the world bearing my grave,
And your eyes open in earth.   You touched my life.
My life reaches the skin, moves under your smile,
And your throat and your shoulders and your face and your
    thighs
Flash.
            I am haunted by interrupted acts,
Introspective as a leper, enchanted
By a repulsive clew,
A gross and fugitive movement of the limbs.
Is this the love that shook the lights to flame?
Sheeted avenues thrash in the wind,
Torn streets, the savage parks.
I am plunged deep.   Must find the midnight cave.

IV—BLACK BLOOD

A habit leading to murder, smoky laughter
Hated at first, but necessary later.
Alteration of motives.   To stamp in terror
Around the deserted harbor, down the hill
Until the woman laced into a harp
Screams and screams and the great clock strikes,
Swinging its giant figures past the face.
The Floating Man rides on the ragged sunset
Asking and asking.   Do not say, Which loved?
Which was beloved? Only, Who most enjoyed?
Armored ghost of rage, screaming and powerless.
Only find me and touch my blood again.
Find me.   A girl runs down the street
Singing Take me, yelling Take me Take
Hang me from the clapper of a bell
And you as hangman ring it sweet tonight,
For nothing clean in me is more than cloud
Unless you call it.   —As I ran I heard
A black voice beating among all that blood:
"Try to live as if there were a God."

V—THE BROKEN WORLD

Came to Ajanta cave, the painted space of the breast,
The real world where everything is complete,
There are no shadows, the forms of incompleteness.
The great cloak blows in the light, rider and horse arrive,
The shoulders turn and every gift is made.
No shadows fall.   There is no source of distortion.
In our world, a tree casts the shadow of a woman,
A man the shadow of a phallus, a hand raised
The shadow of a whip.
Here everything is itself,
Here all may stand
On summer earth.
Brightness has overtaken every light,

And every myth netted itself in flesh.
New origins, and peace given entire
And the spirit alive.
In the shadowless cave
The naked arm is raised.
Animals arrive,
Interlaced, and gods
Interlaced, and men
Flame-woven.
I stand and am complete.
Crawls from the door,
Black at my two feet
The shadow of the world.

World, not yet one,
Enters the heart again.
The naked world, and the old noise of tears,
The fear, the expiation and the love,
A world of the shadowed and alone.

The journey, and the struggles of the moon.

≥ THE MEETING ≥

One o'clock in the letter-box
Very black and I will go home early.
Now I have put off my dancing-dress
And over a sheet of distance write my love.
I walk in the city with my pride of theme
While the lean girls at their betrayal smiling
Dance, do their sea-green dance, and laugh in dancing.
And all the stars fade out of my sky.

Early in the morning on a windy ocean.
My sleep opens upon your face to kiss and find

And take diversion of the meeting waters,
The flameless sky of peace, blue-sided white air.
I leave you as the trivial birds career
In separation, a dream of easy parting.
I see you through a door. The door sails away,
And all the ships move into the real sea.

Let that far day arrive, that evening stain!
Down the alleys of the night I trail a cloak;
Field-dusk and mountain-dusk and final darkness —
Each absence brings me nearer to that night
When I stone-still in desire standing
Shall see the masked body of love enter the garden
To reach the night-burning, the perpetual fountain.
And all the birds fly out of my scene.

❧ DRUNKEN GIRL ❧

Do you know the name of the average animal?
Not the dog,
    Nor the green-beaded frog,
Nor the white ocean monster lying flat —
    Lower than that.
The curling one who comes out in the storm—
The middle one's the worm.

Lift up your face, my love, lift up your mouth,
Kiss me and come to bed
    And do not bow your head
Longer on what is bad or what is good —
    The dead are terribly misunderstood,
And sin and godhead are in the worm's blind eye,
We'll come to averages by and by.

❧ WHO IN ONE LIFETIME ❧

Who in one lifetime sees all causes lost,
Herself dismayed and helpless, cities down,
Love made monotonous fear and the sad-faced
Inexorable armies and the falling plane,
Has sickness, sickness. Introspective and whole,
She knows how several madnesses are born,
Seeing the integrated never fighting well,
The flesh too vulnerable, the eyes tear-torn.

She finds a pre-surrender on all sides:
Treaty before the war, ritual impatience turn
The camps of ambush to chambers of imagery.
She holds belief in the world, she stays and hides
Life in her own defeat, stands, though her whole world
    burn,
A childless goddess of fertility.

❧ LOVE AND ITS
    DOORS AND WINDOWS ❧

History melts my houses,
But they were all one house
Where in the dark beginning
A tall and maniac nurse
Hid tortures behind the door
And afterwards kissed me
Promising all as before.

The second house was music;
The childish hands of fear
Lying on a piano
That was blackness and light,

Opened my life with sound —
Extorting promises
Loud in the ringing air.

After that, broken houses,
The wealthy halls of cloud
Haunted by living parents
And the possessive face.
Power and outrage looking
At the great river
Marvellous filthy and gold.

When love lay in my arms
I all night kissed that mouth,
And the incredible body
Slept warm at my side;
But the walls fell apart
Among my lifetime dream —
O, a voice said crying,
My mother's broken heart.

Nothing was true in the sense
I wanted it to be true.
Victory came late,
Excitement returned too soon.
If my love were for the dead,
Desire would restore
Me to my life again.

My love is for the living;
They point me down to death,
And death I will not take.
My promises have grown,
My kiss was never false,
The faint clear-colored walls
Are not forever down.

❧ LONG PAST MONCADA ❧

Nothing was less than it seemed, my darling:
The danger was greater, the love was greater, the suffering
       Grows daily great—
And the fear we saw gathering into that Spanish valley
Is rank in all countries, a garden of growing death;
Your death, my darling, the threat to our lifetime
       And to all we love.

Whether you fell at Huesca during the lack of guns,
Or later, at Barcelona, as the city fell,
       You reach my days;
Among the heckling of clocks, the incessant failures,
I know how you recognized our war, and ran
To it as a runner to his eager wedding
       Or our immediate love.

If I indeed killed you, my darling, if my cable killed
Arriving the afternoon the city fell,
       No further guilt
Could more irrevocably drive my days
Through the disordered battles and the cities down
In a clash of metal on murder, a stampede of
       Hunger and death.

Other loves, other children, other gifts, as you said,
"Of the revolution," arrive—but, darling, where
       You entered, life
Entered my hours, whether you lie fallen
Among those sunlight fields, or by miracle somewhere stand,
Your words of war and love, death and another promise
       Survive as a lifetime sound.

ᆖ A GAME OF BALL ᆖ

On a ground beaten gold by running and
Over the Aztec crest of the sky and
Past the white religious faces of the
Bulls and far beyond, the ball goes flying.

Sun and moon and all the stars of the moon
Are dancing across our eyes like the flight of armies
And the loser dies. Dark player and bright
Play for the twinned stiff god of life and death.
They die and become the law by which they fight.

Walls grow out of this light, branches out of the stone,
And fire running from the farthest winds
Pours broken flame on these fantastic sands
Where, sunlit, stands the goddess of earth and death,
A frightful peasant with work-hardened hands.

But over the field flash all the colors of summer,
The battle flickers in play, a game like sacrifice.
The sun rides over, the moon and all her stars.
Whatever is ready to eat us, we have found
This place where the gods play out the game of the sky
And bandy life and death across a summer ground.

ᆖ DARKNESS MUSIC ᆖ

The days grow and the stars cross over
And my wild bed turns slowly among the stars.

❧ SONG ❧

The world is full of loss;   bring, wind, my love,
    My home is where we make our meeting-place,
    And love whatever I shall touch and read
    Within that face.

Lift, wind, my exile from my eyes;
    Peace to look, life to listen and confess,
    Freedom to find to find to find
    That nakedness.

ॐ V.
ELEGIES ॐ

For Otto Boch

ও FIRST ELEGY. ROTTEN LAKE ও

As I went down to Rotten Lake I remembered
the wrecked season, haunted by plans of salvage,
snow, the closed door, footsteps and resurrections,
    machinery of sorrow.

The warm grass gave to the feet and the stilltide water
was floor of evening and magnetic light and
reflection of wish, the black-haired beast with my eyes
    walking beside me.

The green and yellow lights, the street of water standing
point to the image of that house whose destruction
I weep, when I weep you.   My door (no), poems, rest,
    (don't say it!) untamable need.

*

When you have left the river you are a little way
nearer the lake;   but I leave many times.
Parents parried my past;   the present was poverty,
the future depended on my unfinished spirit.
There were no misgivings because there was no choice,
only regret for waste, and the wild knowledge:
growth and sorrow and discovery.

When you have left the river you proceed alone;
all love is likely to be illicit;   and few
friends to command the souls;   they are too feeble.
Rejecting the subtle and contemplative minds
as being too thin in the bone;   and the gross thighs
and unevocative hands fail also.   But the poet
and his wife, those who say Survive, remain;
and those two who were with me on the ship
leading me to the sum of the years, in Spain.

When you have left the river you will hear the war.
In the mountains, with tourists, in the insanest groves

the sound of kill, the precious face of peace.
And the sad frightened child, continual minor,
returns, nearer whole circle, O and nearer
all that was loved, the lake, the naked river,
what must be crossed and cut out of your heart,
what must be stood beside and straightly seen.

*

As I went down to Rotten Lake I remembered
how the one crime is need.   The man lifting the loaf
with hunger as motive can offer no alibi, is
     always condemned.

These are the lines at the employment bureau
and the tense students at their examinations;
needing makes clumsy and robs them of their wish,
     in one fast gesture

plants on them failure of the imagination;
and lovers who lower their bodies into the chair
gently and sternly as if the flesh had been wounded,
     never can conquer.

Their need is too great, their vulnerable bodies
rigidly joined will snap, turn love away,
fear parts them, they lose their hands and voices, never
     get used to the world.

Walking at night, they are asked Are you your best friend's
best friend? and must say No, not yet, they are
love's vulnerable, and they go down to Rotten Lake
     hoping for wonders.

Dare it arrive, the day when weakness ends?
When the insistence is strong, the wish converted?
I prophesy the meeting by the water
     of these desires.

I know what this is, I have known the waking
when every night ended in one cliff-dream
of faces drowned beneath the porous rock
    brushed by the sea;

suffered the change : deprived erotic dreams
to images of that small house where peace
walked room to room and always with one face
    telling her stories,

and needed that, past loss, past fever, and the
attractive enemy who in my bed
touches all night the body of my sleep,
    improves my summer

with madness, impossible loss, and the dead music
of altered promise, a room torn up by the roots,
the desert that crosses from the door to the wall,
    continual bleeding,

and all the time that will which cancels enmity,
seeks its own Easter, arrives at the water-barrier;
must face it now, biting the lakeside ground;
    looks for its double,

the twin that must be met again, changeling need,
blazing in color somewhere, flying yellow
into the forest with its lucid edict:
    take to the world,

this is the honor of your flesh, the offering
of strangers, the faces of cities, honor of all your wish.
Immortal undoing! I say in my own voice. These prophecies
    may all come true,

out of the beaten season.   I look in Rotten Lake
wait for the flame reflection, seeing only

the free beast flickering black along my side
    animal of my need,

and cry I want! I want! rising among the world
to gain my converted wish, the amazing desire
that keeps me alive, though the face be still, be still,
the slow dilated heart know nothing but lack,
now I begin again the private rising,
the ride to survival of that consuming bird
beating, up from dead lakes, ascents of fire.

૱ SECOND ELEGY. AGE OF MAGICIANS ૱

A baroque night advances in its clouds,
maps strain loose and are lost, the flash-flood breaks,
the lifting moonflare lights this field a moment,
while death as a skier curves along the snows,
death as an acrobat swings year to year,
turns down to us the big face of a nurse.
Roads open black, and the magicians come.

The aim of magicians is inward pleasure.
The prophet lives by faith and not by sight,
Being a visionary, he is divided,
or Cain, forever shaken by his crime.
Magnetic ecstasy, a trance of doom
mean the magician, worshipping a darkness
with gongs and lurid guns, the colors of force.
He is again the unity of light.

The Magician has his symbols, brings up his children by them:
the march-step, the staircase at night, the long cannon.
The children grow in authority and become
Molitor, Dr. Passavant, powerful Dr. Falcon,

bring their professors, and soon may govern
the zone, the zodiac, the king on his throne.
"Because the age holds its own dangers.
"Because snow comes with lightnings, omens with all seasons."
(The Prophet covers his face against the wall,
weeps, fights to think again, to plan to start
the dragon, the ecliptic, and the heart.)

The Magician lifts himself higher than the world.
The Prophets were more casual. They endured,
and in the passive dread of solitude
heard calls, followed veiled, in midnight humility.
They claimed no preference;   they separated
unity from blindness
living from burning
tribute from tribute.

They have gone under, and do they come again?
The index of prophecy is light
and steeped therein
the world with all its signatures visible.

*

Does this life permit its living to wear strength?
Who gives it, protects it.   It is food.
Who refuses it, it eats in time as food.
It is the world and it eats the world.
Who knows this, knows.   This has been said.

This is the vision in the age of magicians:
it stands at immense barriers, before mountains:
'I came to you in the form of a line of men,
and when you threw down the paper, and when you sat at the play,
and when you killed the spider, and when you saw the shadow
of the fast plane skim fast over your lover's face.
And when you saw the table of diplomats,
the newsreel of ministers, the paycut slip,
the crushed child's head, clean steel, factories,

the chessmen on the marble of the floor,
each flag a country, each chessman a live man,
one side advancing southward to the pit,
one side advancing northward to the lake,
and when you saw the tree, half bright half burning.
You never inquired into these meanings.
If you had done this, you would have been restored.'

The word is war.
And there is a prediction that you are the avenger.

They cut the people's hands, and their shoulders were left,
they cut their feet off, and their thighs were whole,
they cut them down to the torse, but the voice shouted,
they cut the head off, but the heart rang out.

And in the residential districts, where nothing ever happens,
armies of magicians filled the streets,
shouting
Need!   Bread!   Blood!   Death!

And all this is because of you.
And all this is avenged by you.
Your index light, your voice the voice,
your tree half green and half burning,
half dead half bright,
your cairns, your beacons, your tree in green and flames,
unbending smoke in the sky, planes' noise, the darkness,
magic to fight.   Much to restore; now know.   Now be
Seer son of Sight, Hearer, of Ear, at last.

THIRD ELEGY. THE FEAR OF FORM

Tyranny of method!   the outrageous smile
seals the museums, pours a mob skidding
up to the formal staircase, stopped, mouths open.
And do they stare?   They do.
At what?   A sunset?

Blackness, obscurity, bravado were the three colors;
wit-play, movement, and wartime the three moments;
formal groups, fire, facility, the three hounds.

This was their art : a wall daubed like a face,
a penis or finger dipped in a red pigment.
The sentimental frown gave them their praise,
prized the wry color, the twisted definition,
and said,   "You are right to copy."

But the car full of Communists put out hands and guns,
blew 1 – 2 – 3 on the horn before the
surrealist house, a spiral in Cataluña.

New combinations : set out materials now,
combine them again!   the existence is the test.
What do you want?   Lincoln blacking his lessons
in charcoal on an Indiana shovel?
or the dilettante, the impressario's beautiful skull
choosing the tulip crimson satin, the yellow satin
as the ballet dances its tenth time to the mirror?
Or the general's nephew, epaulets from birth,
run down the concourse, shouting Planes for Spain?

New methods, the staring circle given again
force, a phoenix of power, another Ancient
sits in his circle, while the plaster model
of an equation slowly rotates beneath him,
and all his golden compass leans.
Create an anti-sentimental : Sing!

"For children's art is not asylum art,
"there are these formal plays in living, for
"the equal triangle does not spell youth,
"the cube nor age, the sphere nor ever soul.
"Asylum art is never children's art.
"They cut the bones down, but the line remained.
"They cut the line for good, and reached the point
"blazing at the bottom of its night."

*

A man is walking, wearing the world, swearing
saying You damn fools come out into the open.
Whose dislocated wish?   Whose terrors whine?
I'll fuse him straight.
The usable present starts by calendar.

Chorus of bootblacks, printers, collectors of shit
Your witwork works, your artwork shatters, die.
Hammer up your abstractions.   Divide, O zoo.
—He's a queer bird, a hero, a kangaroo.
What is he going to do?

He calls Rise out of cities, you memorable ghosts
scraps of an age whose choice is seen
to lie between evils.   Dazzle-paint the rest,
it burns my eyes with its acetylene.
Look through the wounds, mystic and human fly,
you spiritual unicorn, you clew of eyes.

Ghosts to approach the blood in fifteen cities.
Did you walk through the walls of the Comtesse de Noailles?
Was there a horror in Chicago?
Or ocean?   Or ditches at the road.   Or France,
while bearing guarding shadowing painting in Paris,
Picasso like an ass Picasso like a dragon Picasso like a
romantic movement
and immediately after, stations of swastikas

Prague and a thousand boys swing circles clean
girls by the thousand curve their arms together
geometries of wire
the barbed, starred
Heil

Will you have capitals with their tarnished countesses
their varnished cemetery life
vanished Picassos
or clean acceptable Copenhagen
or by God a pure high monument
white yellow and red
up against Minnesota?

Does the sea permit its dead to wear jewels?

Flame, fusion, defiance are your three guards,
the sphere, the circle, the cluster your three guides,
the bare, the blond and the bland are your three goads.

Adam, Godfinger, only these contacts function:
light and the high accompanied design,
contact of points   the fusion say of sex
the atombuster too along these laws.
Put in a sphere, here, at the focal joint,
he said, put it in.   The moment is arrangement.
Currents washed through it, spun, blew white,
fused.   For! the sphere! proving!

This was the nightmare of a room alone,
the posture of grave figure, finger on other head,
he puts the finger of power on him,
optic of grandiose delusion.
All you adjacent and contagious points,
make room for fusion;   fall,
you monuments, snow on your heads,
your power, your pockets, your dead parts.

Standing at midnight corners under corner-lamps
we wear the coat and the shadow of the coat.
The mind sailing over a scene lets light arrive
conspicuous sunrise, the knotted smoke rising,
the world with all its signatures visible.
Play of materials in balance,
carrying the strain of a new process.
Of the white root, the nature of the base,
contacts, making an index.
And do they stare?   They do.
Our needs, our violences.
At what?   Contortion of body and spirit.
To fuse it straight.

ᢒᤰ FOURTH ELEGY. THE REFUGEES ᢒᤰ

And the child sitting alone planning her hope:
I want to write for my race.   But what race will you speak,
being American?   I want to write for the living.
But the young grow more around us every day.
They show new faces, they come from far, they live
occupied with escape, freeze in the passes, sail
early in the morning.   A few arrive to help.
    Mother, those were not angels, they were knights.

Many are cast out, become artists at rejection.
They saw the chute, the intelligible world
so wild become, it fell, a hairy apparent star
this time with not a public saint in sight
to record miracle.   The age of the masked and the alone begins,
we look for sinister states, a loss shall learning suffer
before the circle of this sun be done,
the palace birds of the new tyrants rise
flying into the wounded sky, sky of catastrophe;

help may be near, but remedy is far,
rain, blood, milk, famine, iron, and epidemic
pour in the sky where a comet drags his tail.
The characters of the spectacles are dead,
nothing is left but ventriloquists and children,
and bodies without souls are not a sacrifice.

It is the children's voyage must be done
before the refugees come home again.
They run like lemmings out
building their suffocated bodies up
to let the full stream pass.
The predatory birds sail over them.
They dash themselves into lighthouses, where the great
    lights hold up,
they laugh at sympathy : "Have you nothing better to do
    in the trenches?"
And at that brink, that bending over doom,
become superior to themselves, in crisis.
There is an addition and fusion of qualities.

They are the children.   They have their games.
They made a circle on a map of time,
skipping they entered it, laughing lifted the agate.
I will get you an orange cat, and a pig called Tangerine.
The gladness-bird beats wings against an opaque glass.
There is a white bird in the top of the tree.
They leave their games, and pass.

Cut.   Frozen and cut.   Off at the ankle.   Off at the hip.
    Off at the knee.   Cut off.
Crossing the mountains many died of cold.

We have spoken of guilt to you too long.
The blame grows on us who carry you the news.
And as the man bringing the story of suicide
lives with the fact, feels murder in himself,
as murderous regents with their gentle kings

know the seductions of crime long before death takes hold,
we bear their—
                            a child crying shrill in a white street
"Aviación!" among the dust of geysers,
the curling rust of Spanish tile.
We bear their smile, we smile under the guilt,
in an access of sickness,   "Let me alone, I'm healthy!"
cry.   And in danger, the sexually witty
speak in short sentences, the unfulfilled.
While definition levels others out.
Wish : the unreality of fulfilled action.
Wish : the reality of fulfilled thought.
Images of luxury.   Image of life.
A phoenix at play among the peonies.
The random torture predicts the random thought.
Over the thought and bird and flowers, the plane.

Coming to strange countries refugee children find
land burned over by winter, a white field and black star
falling like firework where no rockets are
into hell-cities with blank brick and church-bells
(I like this city.   This is a peaceful city)
ringing the bees in the hot garden with their mixing sounds,
ringing the love that falters among these hills,
red-flowering maple and the laugh of peace.
It will take a bell-ringing god tremendous imagined descending
for the healing of hell.

A line of birds, a line of gods.   O bells.
And all the birds have settled on their shadows.
And down the shadowed street a line of children.
You can make out the child ahead of you.
It turns with a gesture that asks for a soft answer.
It sees the smaller child ahead of it.
The child ahead of it turns.   Now, in the close-up
faces throw shadow off.   It is yourself
walks down this street at five-year intervals,
seeing yourself diminishing ahead,

five years younger, and five years younger, and young,
until the farthest infant has a face
ready to grow into any child in the world.

    They take to boats.   The shipwreck of New York.
    To trains whose sets of lines pass along boxes,
    children's constructions.
    Rush to rejection
    foreknowing the steps,
        disfigurement of women, insults of disease,
        negations of power.   They people the earth.
        They are the strong.   They see the enemy.
        They dream the relaxed heart, coming again to power,
        the struggle, the Milk-Tree of Children's Paradise.

They are the real creation of a fictional character.
They fuse a dead world straight.

A line of shadowy children issues, surf issues it,
sickness boiled in their flesh, but they are whole,
insular strength surrounds them, hunger feeds them strong,
the ripened sun finds them, they are the first of the world,
free of the ferryman Nostalgia, who stares at the backward shore.
Growing free of the old in their slow growth of death,
they hold the flaming apples of the spring.
They are exposed to danger.
Ledges of water trick them,
they fall through the raw colors of excavations,
are crushed by monuments, high stone like whale-blow rising,
the backwash of machines can strike them down.
A hill on a map claims them, their procession reaches
a wavy topographical circle where
two gunners lie behind their steelwork margins,
spray shot across the line, do random death.
They fire in a world infected by trenches,
through epidemics of injuries, Madrid, Shanghai,
Vienna, Barcelona, all cities of contagion,
issue survivors from the surf of the age.

Free to be very hungry and very lonely.
And in the countries of the mind, Cut off at the knee.   Cut off
    at the armpit.   Cut off at the throat.
Free to reclaim the world and sow a legend,
to make the adjustments never made,
repair the promises broken and the promise kept.
They blame our lives, lie on our wishes with their eyes our own,
to say and to remember and avenge.   A lullaby for a believing
    child.

ॐ FIFTH ELEGY. A TURNING WIND ॐ

Knowing the shape of the country.   Knowing the midway
                travels of
migrant fanatics, living that life, up with the dawn and
moving as long as the light lasts, and when the sun is falling
    to wait, still standing;

and when the black has come, at last lie down, too tired to
turn to each other, feeling only the land's demand under them.
Shape that exists not as permanent quality, but varies with
    even the movement of bone.

Even in skeletons, it depends on the choices of action.
A definite plan is visible.   We are either free-moving or
fixed to some ground.   The shape has no meaning
    outside of the function.

Fixed to Europe, the distant, adjacent, we lived, with the land-
promise of life of our own.   Course down the East—frontiers
meet you at every turn—the headlights find them, the plain's,
    and the solar cities'

recurrent centers.   And at the middle of the great world the
                wind

answers the shape of the country, a turning traveller
follows the hinge-line of coast, the first indefinite
    axis of symmetry

torn off from sympathy with the past and planted,
a primitive streak prefiguring the west, an ideal
which had to be modified for stability,
    to make it work.

Architecture is fixed not only by present needs but
also by ancestors.   The actual structure means a plan determined
by the nature of ancestors;   its details are determined by
    function and interference.

There are these major divisions : for those attached to the sea-
            floor,
a fan at freedom, flexible, wavering, designed to catch food
from all directions.   For the sedentary, for those who crouch
            and look,
    radial symmetry,

spokes to all margins for support.   For those who want move-
            ment,
this is achieved through bilateral symmetry only,
a spine and straight attack, all muscles working,
    up and alive.

                              *

And there are years of roads, and centuries of need,
of walking along the shadow of a wall, of visiting houses,
hearing the birds trapped in the wall, the framework trembling
    with struggles of birds,

years of nightwalking in stranger cities, relost and unnamed,
recurrent familiar rooms, furnished only with nightmare,
recurrent loves, the glass eye of unreal ambition,
    years of initiation,

of dishallucination on the diamond meadows,
seeing the distances of false capes ahead,
feeling the tide-following and turning wind,
    travelling farther

under abrasive weather, to the bronzy river,
the rust, the brown, the terrible dead swamps,
the hanging moss the color of all the hanged,
    cities whose heels

ring out their news of hell upon all streets,
churches where you betray yourself, pray ended desire,
white wooden houses of village squares.   Always one gesture:
    rejecting of backdrops.

These are the ritual years, whose lore is names of shapes,
Grabtown, Cockade Alley, Skid Row where jobless live,
their emblem a hitch-hiker with lips basted together,
    and marvel rivers,

the flooded James, a double rainbow standing over Richmond,
the remnant sky above the Cape Fear River, blue stain on red
                water,
the Waccamaw with its bone-trees, Piscataqua's rich mouth,
    red Sound and flesh of sand.

—A nation of refugees that will not learn its name;
still shows these mothers enduring, their hidden faces,
the cry of the hurt child at a high night-window,
    hand-to-hand warfare,

the young sitting in libraries at their only rest
or making love in the hallway under an orange bulb,
the boy playing baseball at Hungry Mother State Park,
    bestiaries of cities

and this shape, this meaning that promises seasonal joy.
Whose form is unquietness and yet the seeker of rest,

whose travelling hunger has range enough, its root
    grips through the world.

The austere fire-world of night : Gary or Bethlehem,
in sacred stacks of flame — or stainless morning,
anti-sunlight of lakes' reflection, matchlight on face,
    the thorny light of fireworks

lighting a way for the shape, this country of celebrations
deep in a passage of rebirth.   Adventures of countries,
adventures of travellers, visions, or Christ's adventures
    forever following him

lit by the night-light of history, persevering
into the incredible washed morning air.
The luisarne swamp is our guide and the glare ice,
    the glow of tracklights,

the lights winding themselves into a single beacon,
big whooping riders of night, a wind that whirls
all of our motives into a single stroke,
    shows us a country

of which the birds know mountains that we have not dreamed,
climbing these unsuspected slopes they fade.   Butte and pavil-
               ion
vanish into a larger scape, morning vaults all those hills
    rising on ranges

that stand gigantic on the roots of the world,
where points expand in pleasure of raw sweeping
gestures of joy, whose winds sweep down like stairs,
    and the felled forests

on hurricane ridges show a second growth.   The dances
of turkeys near storm, a pouring light, tornado
umbilical to earth, fountains of rain, a development
    controlled by centers,

until the organs of this anatomy are fleshed away at last
of gross, and determining self, develop a final structure
in isolation.   Masterpieces of happiness arrive,
    alive again in another land,

remembering pain, faces of suffering, but they know growth,
go through the world, hunger and rest desiring life.
Mountains are spines to their conquest, these wrecked houses
    (vines spiral the pillars)

are leaning their splintered sides on tornadoes, lifted careening
in wheels, in whirlwind, in a spool of power
drawing a spiral on the sun, drawing a sign of
    strength on the mountains,

the fusing stars lighting initiated cities.
The thin poor whiteness raining on the ground
forgotten in fickle eclipses, thunderbirds of dream
    following omens,

following charts of the moving constellations.
Charts of the country of all visions, imperishable
stars of our old dream : process, which having neither
    sorrow nor joy

remains as promise, the embryo in the fire.
The tilted cities of America, fields of metal,
the seamless wheatfields, the current of cities running
    below our wings

promise that knowledge of systems which may bless.
May permit knowledge of self, a lover's wish of conversion
until the time when the dead lake rises in light,
the shape is organized in travelling space,
this hope of travel, to find the place again,
rest in the triumph of the reconceived,
lie down again together face to face.

❧ SIXTH ELEGY. RIVER ELEGY ❧

In burning summer I saw a season of betrayal,
the world fell away, and wasteful climbing green
covered the breaking of bodies, covered our hearts.
Unreal in the burning, many-motioned life
lay like a sea, but fevers found my grief,
I turned in that year to retrieve the stainless river,
the lost, the flowing line of escaped music.

Year of judgment! Century of betrayal!
They built their cities on the banks of war
and all their cities are down, the Floating Man
swims in the smoke of their sky, the Double Woman
smiles up through the water with her distorted mouth.
I stand over reflection as the world darkens in
destruction of countries, all souls downward set,
life narrowing to one color of a choked river
and hell on both its banks.   My city, my city!
They never built cities.   Cities are for the living.
They built for the half-dead and the half-alive.
Their history is a half-history.   And we go down.
They built their villages whose lame towers fell
where error was overgrown until the long
tentacular ruin touches all fields.   My love!
Did I in that country build you villages?
Great joy my love, even there, until they fell
and green betrayal climbed over the wall.

Defeat and raging and a burning river.
Half-faced, half-sexed, the living dead arrive
passing, a lip, a breast, half of a hand.
Gaudy sadistic streets, dishonest avenues
where every face has bargained for its eyes.
And they come down to the river, driven down.
And all the faces fly out of my city.
The rich streets full of empty coats parading
and one adolescent protesting violin,

the slum full of their flayed and faceless bodies,
they shiver, they are working to buy their skin.
They are lost. They come down to look for life in a river,
plunge, turn and plunge, they cannot change their life,
swimming, their head is in another world.

World without form.   Chaos beaten and beaten,
raging and suffering and hoping to take shape.
I saw your summer.   I saw your river flow.
I being wasted everywhere saw waste.
Hell's entropy at work and torment general,
friend against most-known friend, love fighting off love.
They asked for an end to emptiness; their sick throats
      filled with foam,
prayed to be solved, and rose to deal betrayal.
And I falling through hell passed many friends, and love,
and a haunted woman warned me as I fell.
Downward through currents, the horrors with little hands.

The chaos, the web of the heart, this bleeding knot;
raises me swimming now, one moment in the air
and light is on my face, the fans over the river
of wind, of goodness.   Lie gasping on this shore,
there is nothing in the world but an honest word
which the severed away may speak before we die.
Let me tell you what I have held to all along:
when I said that I loved you, when I crossed the frontier,
when I learned the obscurities of a frightened child,
when I shut the door, and felt the sprouting tears,
when I saw the river, when I learned resurrection,
the joy of your hands in a pain that called More Life.
Let me tell you what I have meant all along:
meaning of poetry and personal love,
a world of peace and freedom, man's need recognized,
and all the agonies that will begin that world.

Betrayed, we are betrayed.   The set of the great faces
mean it, the following eyes.   They are the flayed men,

their strength is at the center, love and the time's disease
lie at their skin.   The kiss in the flaring garden
when all the trees closed in.   The knotted terrible lips.
The black blood risen and the animal rage.
The last fierce accident, whose back-thrown drowning head
among the escaping sound of water hears
slows insane music groping for a theme.

My love, reach me again.   The smell of the sea,
wind-flower, sea-flower, the fallen gull-feather.
Clear water and order and an end to dreams:
ether-dreams, surrounded beasts, the aftertoll of fear,
the world reduced to a rising line of water,
the patient deserted by the analyst.
To keep the knowledge that holds my race alive:
spiritual grace of the material world.

I walked under the sky, and the high clouds
hollowed in ribs arched over their living heart:
the world, the corporeal world that will not die.
No, world's no heart—here is yourself walking
in a cage of clouds looking up wanting one face
over you and that look to fill the sky.
Carrying counter-agony into the world,
dream-singing, river-madness, the tragic fugal love
of a theme balancing another theme.

Disorder of suffering, a flight of details, a world
with no shadows at noontime and never at night a light.
Suddenly the flame-blue of a drunken sky
and it is the change, the reds and metals of autumn.
But I curse autumn, for I do not change,
I love, I love, and we are far from peace,
and the great river moves unbearably;
actual gestures of giving, and I may not give.
Water will hold my shadows, the kiss of darkness,
maternal death's tender and delicate promises
seethe at the lips, release and the full sleep.

Even now the bright corporeal hand
might come to redeem the long moment of dying.
Even now if I could rest my life,
my forehead on those knees and the arriving shadows
in rising quiet as the long night arrives.
Terror, war, terror, black blood and wasted love.
The most terrible country, in the heads of men.
This is the war imagination made;
it must be strong enough to make a peace.
My peace is strong enough if it will come
flowing, the color of eyes.   When the world burns away
nothing is left can ever be betrayed.

All broken promises, adulterate release—
cast in the river Death, charred surface of waste,
a downward soulset, never the old heaven
held for a moment as breath held underwater;
but we must rise into a breathing world.
And this dark bellowing century, on its knees—?
If all this must go down, it must.
And all this brilliance go to dust?
Only the meanings can remain alive.
When the cemeteries are military objectives
and love's a downward drawing at the heart
and every letter bears the stamp of death.

There is no solution.   There is no happiness.
Only the range must be taken, a way be found to use
the inmost frenzy and the outer doom.
They are here, they run their riot in the clouds,
fly in our blood and over all our mountains,
corrupt all waters, poison the pride of theme.

Years of judgment!   Century screaming for
the flowing, the life, the intellectual leap
of waters over a world grown old and wild,
a broken crying for seasonal change until
O God my love in time the waste become
the sure magnificent music of the defeated heart.

ဆ SEVENTH ELEGY. DREAM-
SINGING ELEGY ဆ

Darkness, giving us dream's black unity.
Images in procession start to flow
among the river-currents down the years of judgment
and past the cities to another world.

There are flat places.   After the waterfall
arched like the torso of love, after the voices
singing behind the waterfall, after the water
lying like a lover on the heart,
there is defeat.

And moving through our spirit in the night
memories of these places.
Not ritual, not nostalgia, but our cries,
the axe at the heart, continual rebirth,
the crying of our raw desire,
young.   O many-memoried America!

*

In defeat there are no prophets and no magicians,
only the look in the loved and tortured eyes
when every fantasy restores, and day denies.
The act of war debased to the act of treason
in an age of treason.   We were strong at the first.
We resisted.   We did not plan enough.   We killed.
But the enemy came like thunder in the wood,
a storm over the treetops like a horse's head
reared to a great galloping, and war
trampled us down.   We lost our young men in the fighting,
we lost our homeland, our crops went under the frost,
our children under the hunger.   Now we stand
around this fire, our black hills far behind,
black water far before us, a glitter of time on the sea,
glitter of fire on our faces, the still faces—

stillness waiting for dreams
and only the shadows moving,
shadows and revelations.

In the spring of the year, this new fighting broke out.
No, when the fields were blond.   No, the leaves crimson.
When the old fighting was over, we knew what we were
seeing as if for a first time our dark hills masked with green,
our blond fields with the trees flame-shaped and black
in burning darkness on the unconsumed.
Seeing for a first time the body of our love,
our wish and our love for each other.
Then word came from a runner, a stranger:
"They are dancing to bring the dead back, in the mountains."
We danced at an autumn fire, we danced the old hate and change,
the coming again of our leaders.   But they did not come.
Our singers lifted their arms, and a singer cried,
"You must sing like me and believe, or be turned to rock!"

The winter dawned, but the dead did not come back.
News came on the frost, "The dead are on the march!"
We danced in prison to a winter music,
many we loved began to dream of the dead.
They made no promises, we never dreamed a threat.
And the dreams spread.

But there were no armies, and the dead were dead,
there was only ourselves, the strong and symbol self
dreaming among defeat, our torture and our flesh.
We made the most private image and religion,
stripped to the last resistance of the wish,
remembering the fighting and the lava beds,
the ground that opened, the red wounds opening,
remembering the triumph in the night,
the big triumph and the little triumph—
wide singing and the battle-flash—
assassination and whisper.

In the summer, dreaming was common to all of us,
the drumbeat hope, the bursting heart of wish,
music to bind us as the visions streamed
and midnight brightened to belief.
In the morning we told our dreams.
They all were the same dream.

Dreamers wake in the night and sing their songs.
In the flame-brilliant midnight, promises
arrive, singing to each of us with tongues of flame:
"We are hopes, you should have hoped us,
We are dreams, you should have dreamed us."
Calling our name.

When we began to fight, we sang hatred and death.
The new songs say, "Soon all people on earth
will live together."   We resist and bless
and we begin to travel from defeat.
Now, as you sing your dream, you ask the dancers,
in the night, in the still night, in the night,
"Do you believe what I say?"
And all the dancers answer "Yes."

To the farthest west, the sea and the striped country
and deep in the camps among the wounded cities
half-world over, the waking dreams of night
outrange the horrors.   Past fierce and tossing skies
the rare desires shine in constellation.
I hear your cries, you little voices of children
swaying wild, nightlost, in black fields calling.
I hear you as the seething dreams arrive
over the sea and past the flaming mountains.
Now the great human dream as great as birth or death,
only that we are not given to remember birth,
only that we are not given to hand down death,
this we hand down and remember.

Brothers in dream, naked-standing friend
rising over the night, crying aloud,
beaten and beaten and rising from defeat,
crying as we cry : We are the world together.
Here is the place in hope, on time's hillside,
where hope, in one's image, wavers for the last time
and moves out of one's body up the slope.
That place in love, where one's self, as the body of love,
moves out of the old lifetime towards the beloved.
Singing.

Who looks at the many colors of the world
knowing the peace of the spaces and the eyes of love,
who resists beyond suffering, travels beyond dream,
knowing the promise of the night-flowering worlds
sees in a clear day love and child and brother
living, resisting, and the world one world
dreaming together.

∾ EIGHTH ELEGY. CHILDREN'S ELEGY ∾

Yes, I have seen their eyes.   In peaceful gardens
the dark flowers now are always children's eyes,
full-colored, haunted as evening under fires
showered from the sky of a burning country.

Shallow-featured children under trees
look up among green shadows of the leaves.
The angel, flaming, gives — into his hands
all is given and he does not change.
The child changes and takes.
All is given.   He makes and changes.
The angel stands.

114 ∾

A flame over the tree.   Night calling in the cloud.
And shadow among winds.   Where does the darkness lie?
It comes out of the person, says the child.
A shadow tied and alive, trying to be.

In the tremendous child-world, everything is high,
active and fiery, sun-cats run through the walls,
the tree blows overhead like a green joy,
and cloudy leopards go hunting in the sky.

The shadow in us sings, "Stand out of the light!"
But I live, I live, I travel in the sun.

On burning voyages of war they go.
Like starving ghosts they stumble after nuns.
Children of heroes, Defeat the dark companion.
But if they are told they are happy, they will know.

Who kills the father burns up the children's tears.
Some suffering blazes beyond all human touch,
some sounds of suffering cry, far out of reach.
These children bring to us their mother's fears.

Singing, "O make us strong O let us go—"
The new world comes among the old one's harms,
old world carrying new world in her arms.
But if you say they are free, then they will know.

War means to me, sings a small skeleton,
only the separation,
mother no good and gone,
taken away in lines of fire and foam.
The end of war
will bring me, bring me home.

The children of the defeated, sparrow-poor and starved,
create, create, must make their world again.
Dead games and false salutes must be their grace.

One wish must move us, flicker from our lives
to the marred face.

My child, my victim, my wish this moment come!
But the martyr-face cries to us fiercely
"I search to learn the way out of childhood;
I need to fight.   I wish, I wish for home."

This is what they say, who were broken off from love:
However long we were loved, it was not long enough.

We were afraid of the broad big policeman,
of lions and tigers, the dark hall and the moon.

After our father went, nothing was ever the same,
when mother did not come back, we made up a war game.

My cat was sitting in the doorway when the planes
went over, and my cat saw mother cry;
furry tears, fire fell, wall went down;
did my cat see mother die?

Mother is gone away, my cat sits here coughing.
I cough and sit.   I am nobody's nothing.

However long they loved us, it was not long enough.
For we have to be strong, to know what they did, and then
our people are saved in time, our houses built again.

You will not know, you have a sister and brother;
my doll is not my child, my doll is my mother.

However strong we are, it is not strong enough.
I want to grow up.   To come back to love.

*

I see it pass before me in parade,
my entire life as a procession of images.
The toy, the golden kernel, the glass lamp.

The present she gave me, the first page I read,
the little animal, the shadowless tall angel.

The angel stands.   The child changes and takes.
He makes a world, stands up among the cousins,
cries to the family, "Ladies and gentlemen—
The world is falling *down!*"   After the smooth hair
darkens, and summer lengthens the smooth cheek,
and the diffuse gestures are no longer weak,
he begins to be the new one, to have what happened,
to do what must be done.

O, when the clouds and the blue horse of childhood
melt away and the golden weapons,
and we remember the first public day's
drums and parades and the first angel
standing in the garden, his dark lips
and silver blood, how he stood,
giving, for all he was was given.

I begin to have what happened to me.

O, when the music of carousels and stars
is known, and the music of the scene
makes a clear meeting, greeting and claim of gods,
we see through the hanging curtain of the year
they change each other with one change of love!
see, in one breath, in a look!
See, in pure midnight a flare of broken color
clears to a constellation.
Peace is asleep, war's lost.   It is love.
I wanted to die.   The masked and the alone
seemed the whole world, and all the gods at war,
and all the people dead and depraved.   Today
the constellation and the music!   Love.

You who seeking yourself arrive at these lines,
look once, and you see the world,
look twice and you see your self.

And all the children moving in their change.

To have what has happened, the pattern and the shock;
and all of them walk out of their childhood,
give to you one blue look.

And all the children bowing in their game,
saying Farewell, Goodbye;   Goodbye, Farewell.

NINTH ELEGY. THE ANTAGONISTS

Pieces of animals, pieces of all my friends
prepare assassinations while I sleep.
They shape my being, a gallery of lives
fighting within me, and all unreconciled.
Before them move my waking dreams, and ways
of the spirit, and simple action.   Among these
I can be well and holy.   Torn by them I am wild,
smile, and revenge myself upon my friends
and find myself among my enemies.
But all these forms of incompleteness pass
out of their broken power to a place
where dream and dream meet and resolve in grace.

The closing of this conflict is the end
of the initiation.   I have known the cliff
and known the cliff-dream of the faces drowned.
Stood in the high sun, a dark girl looking down,
seeing the colors of water swaying beneath me, dense
in the flood-summer, various as my love
and like my hope enchanted.   Drawn to blue
chance and horizons, and back as sea-grasses move
drawn landward slowly by incoming tides—
and then the final cancelling and choice,

not tilted as flowers under wind, but deep
blessing of root and heart, underwater swung,
wrenched, swayed, and given fully to the sea.
Heaven not of rest, but of intensity.

The forms of incompleteness in our land
pass from the eastern and western mountains where
the seas meet the dark islands, where the light
glitters white series on the snowlands, pours its wine
of lenient evening to the center.   Green
on shadows of Indiana, level yellow miles . . .
The prairie emblems and the slopes of the sky
and desert stars enlarging in the frost
redeems us like our love and will not die.
All origins are here, and in this range
the changing spirit can make itself again,
continually love, continually change.

> Out of the myth the mother leaned;
> From out the mother shines the child;
> Man rises, in the mass contained;
> And from this growth creation grows.
> The fire through all the spiral flows:
> Create the creative, many-born!
> And use your love, unreconciled!

*

In wheels, in whirlwind, in a storm of power
alive again and over every land
the thunderbird with lightnings at his wrists.
Eclipses uncloud and show us miracle,
gleaming, our ancestors, all antagonists:
Slave and Conquistador, dead hand-to-hand,
scented fastidious Tory with his whore,
distinguished rebel and woman at the plow.
The fiery embryo umbilical
always to failure, and form developing
American out of conflict.

Fierce dissenting ghosts,
the second Adams' fever and eagle voice
and Jackson's muscular democratic sense.
Sprung in one birth John Brown, a mad old man
whose blood in a single broken gesture freed
many beliefs;   and Lincoln's agony
condemning and confirming.   O, they cry,
the oppositions cry, O fight for me!
Fight, you are bound to freedom, and be free!
When Hawthorne saw the fabulous gift, he tore
flesh from his guilt, and found more guilt;   the bells
rang barter of the self, but Melville drowned.
The doubled phantoms bring to our terrible
chaos the order of a meeting-place
where the exchange is made, the agonies
lie down at last together face to face.

In the black night of blood, the forms begin
to glitter alive, fathers of constellations,
the shining and the music moving on.
We are bound by the deepest feuds to unity.
To make the connections and be born again,
create the creative, that will love the world.

*

Not glistening Indies, not continents, but the world
opening now, and the greatness of our age
that makes its own antagonists of the wish.
We want to find and will spend our lives in finding:
the landfall of our broken voyages
is still our America of contradictions.
Ancestors of that dream lie coupled in our flesh,
pieces of animals, pieces of all our friends
meet in us and we live.   We do not die.

Magical keen Magellan sought a rose
among the compass and legendary winds.
Green sequels rocked his eyes in water;   he

hung with the scorpion sun on noon's glass wall,
stared down, down into the future as he sailed.
Fanatic travels, recurrent mysteries.
Those who want the far shore spend their lives on the ocean.
The hand of God flowers in coasts for these.

Those who want only home spend their lives in the sky.
Flying over tonight, while thirteen searchlights join
high incandescent asters on black air.
The blinding center fastens on a plane
floating and white, glare-white; he wanting land
and intimate fertile hours, hangs there.   Sails
great scends of danger, or wades through crazy sand.

Those who most long for peace now pour their lives on war.
Our conflicts carry creation and its guilt,
these years' great arms are full of death and flowers.
A world is to be fought for, sung, and built:
Love must imagine the world.
                              The wish for love
moving upon the body of love describes
closing of conflict, repeats the sacred ways
in which the spirit dances and survives.

To that far meeting-place call home the enemies—
they keep their oppositions, for the strong
ironic joy of old intensities
still carries virile music.
                              O, the young
will come up
              after us
                        and make the dream,
the real world of our myth.
                              But now, the song
they will discover is a shadowy theme—

Today we are bound, for freedom binds us—we
live out the conflict of our time, until

Love, finding all the antagonists in the dance,
moved by its moods and given to its grace,
resolves the doom
                    and the deliverance.

❧ TENTH ELEGY. ELEGY IN JOY ❧

Now green, now burning, I make a way for peace.
After the green and long beyond my lake,
among those fields of people, on these illuminated
hills, gold, burnt gold, spilled gold and shadowed blue,
the light of enormous flame, the flowing light of the sea,
where all the lights and nights are reconciled.
The sea at last, where all the waters lead.
And all the wars to this peace.

For the sea does not lie like the death you imagine;
this sea is the real sea, here it is.
This is the living.   This peace is the face of the world,
a fierce angel who in one lifetime lives
fighting a lifetime, dying as we all die,
becoming forever, the continual god.

Years of our time, this heart!   The binding of the alone,
bells of all loneliness, binding our lands and our music,
branches full of motion each opening its own flower,
lands of all song, each speaking in his own voice.
Praise in every grace
among the old same war.

Years of betrayal, million death breeding its weaknesses
and hope, buried more deep more black than dream.
Every elegy is the present : freedom eating our hearts,
death and explosion, and the world unbegun.

Now burning and unbegun, I sing earth with its war,
and God the future, and the wish of man.

✻

Though you die, your war lives : the years fought it,
fusing a dead world straight.

The living will be giving you your meanings,
widening to love because of the love of man.
All the wounds crying
I feare, and hope : I burne, and frese like yse . . .
saying to the beloved
For your sake I love cities,
on your love I love the many,
saying to the people,
for your sake I love the world.
The old wounds crying
I find no peace, and all my warres are done.

> Out of our life the living eyes
> See peace in our own image made,
> Able to give only what we can give:
> Bearing two days like midnight.   "Live,"
> The moment offers;   the night requires
> Promise effort love and praise.

Now there are no maps and no magicians.
No prophets but the young prophet, the sense of the world.
The gift of our time, the world to be discovered.
All the continents giving off their several lights,
the one sea, and the air.   And all things glow.

Move as this sea moves, as water, as force.
Peace shines from its life, its war can become
at any moment the fierce shining of peace,
and all the life-night long many voices are saying
The name of all things is Glowing.

123 ৡ

A beginning, a moment of rest that imagines.
And again I go wandering far and alone,
I rise at night, I start up in the silence—
lovely and silver-black the night remembers.
In the cities of America I make my peace;
among the bombs and commands,
the sound that war makes
NO   NO
We see their weeping and their lifetime dreams.

All this, they say to us, because of you.
Much to begin.   Now be your green, your burning,
bear also our joy, come to our meeting-place
and in the triumph of the reconceived
lie down at last together face to face.

*

We tell beginnings : for the flesh and answer,
for the look, the lake in the eye that knows,
for the despair that flows down in widest rivers,
cloud of home;   and also the green tree of grace,
all in the leaf, in the love that gives us ourselves.

The word of nourishment passes through the women,
soldiers and orchards rooted in constellations,
white towers, eyes of children:
saying in time of war What shall we feed?
I cannot say the end.

Nourish beginnings, let us nourish beginnings.
Not all things are blest, but the
seeds of all things are blest.
The blessing is the seed.

This moment, this seed, this wave of the sea, this look, this
        instant of love.
Years over wars and an imagining of peace.   Or the expiation
        journey

toward peace which is many wishes flaming together,
fierce pure life, the many-living home.
Love that gives us ourselves, in the world known to all
new techniques for the healing of a wound,
and the unknown world.   One life, or the faring stars.

❧ VI.
From THE GREEN WAVE ❧

WATER NIGHT

The sky behind the farthest shore
Is darker than I go to sleep.

Blackness of water, the crater at the core,
The many blacknesses begin to gleam.

Rivers of darkness bind me to this land
While overhead the moon goes far to shine,

And now nothing nobody is my own.
The motion of streams glitters before my eyes:

Sources and entrances, they lie no more,
Now darkly keep, now flow now bright

Until all wandering end, a hand
Shine, and the leadings homeward of delight

Seem to begin my deepest sleep
To make a lake of dream.

EYES OF NIGHT-TIME

On the roads at night I saw the glitter of eyes:
my dark around me let shine one ray;   that black
allowed their eyes : spangles in the cat's, air in the moth's
   eye shine,
mosaic of the fly, ruby-eyed beetle, the eyes that never weep,
the horned toad sitting and its tear of blood,
fighters and prisoners in the forest, people
aware in this almost total dark, with the difference,
the one broad fact of light.

Eyes on the road at night, sides of a road like rhyme;
the floor of the illumined shadow sea
and shallows with their assembling flash and show
of sight, root, holdfast, eyes of the brittle stars.
And your eyes in the shadowy red room,
scent of the forest entering, various time
calling and the light of wood along the ceiling
and over us birds calling and their circuit eyes.
And in our bodies the eyes of the dead and the living
giving us gifts at hand, the glitter of all their eyes.

ᢒᣔ SALAMANDER ᢒᣔ

Red leaf.   And beside it, a red leaf alive
flickers, the eyes set wide in the leaf head,
small broad chest, a little taper of flame for tail
moving a little among the leaves like fear.

Flickering red in the wet week of rain
while a bird falls safely through his mile of air.

ᢒᣔ THE MOTIVE OF ALL OF IT ᢒᣔ

The motive of all of it was loneliness,
All the panic encounters and despair
Were bred in fear of the lost night, apart,
Outlined by pain, alone.   Promiscuous
As mercy.   Fear-led and led again to fear
At evening toward the cave where part fire, part
Pity lived in that voluptuousness
To end one and begin another loneliness.

This is the most intolerable motive : this
Must be given back to life again,
Made superhuman, made human, out of pain
Turned to the personal, the pure release:
The rings of Plato and Homer's golden chain
Or Lenin with his cry of Dare We Win.

❧ GREEN LIMITS ❧

My limits crowd around me
like years, like those I loved
whose narrow hope could never
carry themselves.

My limits stand beside me
like those two widowed aunts
who from an empty beach
tore me into the wave.

Green over my low head
the surf threw itself down
tall as my aunts whose hands
locked me past help.

The sand was far behind
and rushing underfoot
water and fear and childhood,
surf of love.

Green limits walled me, water
stood higher than I saw—
glass walls, fall back! let me
dive and be saved.

My limits stand inside me
forever like that wave
on which I ride at last
over and under me.

❧ MRS. WALPURGA ❧

In wet green midspring, midnight and the wind
floodladen and ground-wet, and the immense dry moon.
Mrs. Walpurga under neon saw
the fluid airs stream over fluid evening,
ground, memory, give way and rivers run
into her sticky obsessive kiss of branches,
kiss of a real and visionary mouth,
the moon, the mountain, the round breast's sleepless eye.

Shapes of her fantasy in music from the bars,
swarming like juke-box lights the avenues;
no longer parked in the forest, from these cars,
these velvet rooms and wooden tourist camps,
sheetless under the naked white of the moon.
Wet gaze of eye, plum-color shadow and young
streams of these mouths, the streaming surface of earth
flowing alive with water, the egg and its becoming.

Coming in silence.   The shapes of every dread
seducing the isolated will.   They do not care.
They are not tortured, not tired, not alone.
They break to an arm, a leg, half of a mouth,
kissing disintegrate, flow whole, couple again;
she is changed along, she is a stream in a stream.

These are her endless years, woman and child, in dream
molded and wet, a bowl growing on a wheel,

not mud, not bowl, not clay, but this *becoming,*
winter and split of darkness, years of wish.
To want these couples, want these coupling pairs,
emblems of many parents, of the bed,
of love divided by dream, love with his dead wife,
love with her husband dead, love with his living love.

Mrs. Walpurga cries out : "It is not true!"
The light shifts, flowing away.   "It was never like—"
She stops, but nothing stops.   It moves.   It moves.
And not like anything.   And it is true.
The shapes disfigure.   Here is the feature man,
not whole, he is detail, he gleams and goes.
Here is the woman all cloth, black velvet face,
black, head to ground, close black fit to the skin,
slashed at the mouth and eyes, slashed at the breasts,
slashed at the triangle, showing rose everywhere.

Nights are disturbed, here is a crying river
running through years, here is the flight among
all the Objects of Love.   This wish, this gesture
irresisted, immortal seduction!   The young sea
streams over the land of dream, and there
the mountain like a mist-flower, the dark upright peak.
And over the sheet-flood Mrs. Walpurga
in whitened cycles of her changing moon.

The silence and the music change;   this song
rises and sharps, and never quite can scream—
but this is laughter harsher than nakedness
can take — in the shady shady grove the leaves
move over, the men and women move and part,
the river braids and unfolds in mingling song;
and here is the rain of summer from the moon,
relenting, wet, and giving life at last,
and Mrs. Walpurga and we may wake.

🐦 FOGHORN IN HORROR 🐦

I know that behind these walls is the city, over these rooftops is
the sun.
But I see black clothes only and white clothes with the fog running
in all their shadows.
Every minute the sound of the harbor
intruding on horror with a bellow of horror:
blu-a!   blu-aa!   Ao. . . .

I try to write to you, but here too I meet failure.
It has a face like mine.
Silence and in me and over the water
only the bellowing,
Niobe howling for her life and her children.
Did you think this sorrow of women was a graceful thing?
Horrible Niobe down on her knees:
Blu-a!   Blu-aa!   Ao. . . .

Thirty years, and my full strength, and all I touch has failed.
I sit and see
the black clothes on the line are beautiful, the sky drifting away.
The white clothes of the fog beyond me, beautiful and the shadows.
Blu-aa!   Blu-aa!   Ao.

🐦 SUMMER, THE SACRAMENTO 🐦

To this bridge the pale river and flickers away in images of blue.
And is gone.   While behind me the stone mountains
stand brown with blue lights;   at my right shoulder standing
Shasta, in summer standing, blue with her white lights
near a twilight summer moon, whiter than snow
where the light of evening changes among these legends.

Under me islands lie green, planted with green feathers,
green growing, shadowy grown, gathering streams of the green
    trees.
A hundred streams full of shadows and your upland source
pulled past sun-islands, green in this light as grace,
risen from your sun-mountains where your voices go
returning to water and music is your face.

Flows to the flower-haunted sea, naming and singing, under my
    eyes
coursing, the day of the world.   And the time of my spirit
    streams
before me, slow autumn colors, the cars of a long train;
earth-red, earth-orange, leaf, rust, twilight of earth
stream past the evening river and over into the dark of north,
stream slow like wishes continuing toward those snows.

“ EASTER EVE ”

Wary of time O it seizes the soul tonight
I wait for the great morning of the west
confessing with every breath mortality.
Moon of this wild sky struggles to stay whole
and on the water silvers the ships of war.
I go alone in the black-yellow light
all night waiting for day, while everywhere the sure
death of light, the leaf's sure return to the root
is repeated in million, death of all man to share.
Whatever world I know shines ritual death,
wide under this moon they stand gathering fire,
fighting with flame, stand fighting in their graves.
All shining with life as the leaf, as the wing shines,
the stone deep in the mountain, the drop in the
    green wave.

Lit by their energies, secretly, all things shine.
Nothing can black that glow of life;   although
     each part go crumbling down
     itself shall rise up whole.

Now I say there are new meanings;   now I name
death our black honor and feast of possibility
to celebrate casting of life on life. This earth-long
     day
between blood and resurrection where we wait
remembering sun, seed, fire;   remembering
that fierce Judaean Innocent who risked
every immortal meaning on one life.
Given to our year as sun and spirit are,
as seed we are blessed only in needing freedom.
Now I say that the peace the spirit needs is peace,
not lack of war, but fierce continual flame.
For all men : effort is freedom, effort's peace,
it fights. And along these truths the soul goes home,
     flies in its blazing to a place
     more safe and round than Paradise.

Night of the soul, our dreams in the arms of dreams
dissolving into eyes that look upon us.
Dreams the sources of action, the meeting and the end,
a resting-place among the flight of things.
And love which contains all human spirit, all wish,
the eyes and hands, sex, mouth, hair, the whole woman —
fierce peace I say at last, and the sense of the world.
In the time of conviction of mortality
whatever survive, I remember what I am. —
The nets of this night are on fire with sun and moon
pouring both lights into the open tomb.
Whatever arise, it comes in the shape of peace,
fierce peace which is love, in which move all the stars,
and the breathing of universes, filling, falling away,
and death on earth cast into the human dream.

What fire survive forever
myself is for my time.

❧ NINE POEMS
FOR THE UNBORN CHILD ❧

I.

The childless years alone without a home
Flashed daily with the world's glimpse, happiness.
Always behind was the dark screen of loss
Hardly moving, like heavy hardly-moving cloud.
"Give me myself," or "Take me," I said aloud;
There was little to give, and always less to take.
Except the promise, except the promise darkness
Makes, night and daylight, miracle to come.

Flying over, I suddenly saw the traces
Of man : where man is, you may read the wind
In shadow and smoke, know how the wind is gone
And know the way of man;   in the fall of the plane
Into its levels, encounter the ancient spaces:
The fall to life, the cliff and strait of bone.

II.

They came to me and said, "There is a child."
Fountains of images broke through my land.
My swords, my fountains spouted past my eyes
And in my flesh at last I saw.   Returned
To when we drove in the high forest, and earth
Turned to glass in the sunset where the wild
Trees struck their roots as deep and visible
As their high branches, the double planted world.

"There is no father," they came and said to me.
—I have known fatherless children, the searching, walk
The world, look at all faces for their father's life.
Their choice is death or the world.   And they do choose.
Earn their brave set of bone, the seeking marvelous look
Of those who lose and use and know their lives.

III.

There is a place.   There is a miracle.
I know the nightmare, the black and bone piano,
The statues in the kitchen, a house dissolving in air.
I know the lilac-turreted cathedral
Taking its roots from willows that changed before my eyes
When all became real, real as the sound of bells.
We earthly are aware of transformation;
Miraculously, life, from the old despair.

The wave of smooth water approaches on the sea-
Surface, a live wave individual
Linking, massing its color.   Moving, is struck by wind,
Ribbed, steepened, until the slope and ridge begin;
Comes nearer, brightens.   Now curls, its vanishing
Hollows darken and disappear;   now high above
Me, the scroll, froth, foam of the overfall.

IV.

Now the ideas all change to animals
Loping and gay, now all the images
Transform to leaves, now all these screens of leaves
Are flowing into rivers, I am in love
With rivers, these changing waters carry voices,
Carry all children;   carry all delight.
The water-soothed winds move warm above these waves.
The child changes and moves among these waves.

The waves are changing, they tremble from waves of waters
To other essentials — they become waves of light

And wander through my sleep and through my waking,
And through my hands and over my lips and over
Me;   brilliant and transformed and clear,
The pure light.   Now I am light and nothing more.

V.

Eating sleep, eating sunlight, eating meat,
Lying in the sun to stare
At deliverance, the rapid cloud,
Gull-wing opposing sun-bright wind,
I see the born who dare
Walk on green, walk against blue,
Move in the nightlong flare
Of love on darkness, traveling
Among the rings of light to simple light,
From nowhere to nowhere.
And in my body feel the seasons grown.
Who is it in the dim room?   Who is there?

VI.

Death's threat!   Today I have known laughter
As if for the first time;   have seen into your eyes,
Death, past the still gaze, and found two I love.
One chose you gladly with a laugh advancing,
His hand full of guns, on the enemy in Spain.
The other living with the choice of life
Turning each day of living to the living day.
The strength, the grossness, spirit and gall of choice.

They came to me and said, "If you must choose,
Is it yourself or the child?"   Laughter I learned
In that moment, laughter and choice of life.
I saw an immense ship trembling on the water
Lift by a gesture of hands.   I saw a child.   I saw
A red room, the eyes, the hands, the hands and eyes.

VII.

You will enter the world where death by fear and explosion
Is waited;   longed for by many;   by all dreamed.
You will enter the world where various poverty
Makes thin the imagination and the bone.
You will enter the world where birth is walled about,
Where years are walled journeys, death a walled-in act.
You will enter the world which eats itself
Naming faith, reason, naming love, truth, fact.

You in your dark lake moving darkly now
Will leave a house that time makes, times to come
Enter the present, where all the deaths and all
The old betrayals have come home again.
World where again Judas, the little child,
May grow and choose.   You will enter the world.

VIII.

Child who within me gives me dreams and sleep,
Your sleep, your dreams;   you hold me in your flesh
Including me where nothing has included
Until I said : I will include, will wish
And in my belly be a birth, will keep
All delicacy, all delight unclouded.

Dreams of an unborn child move through my dreams,
The sun is not alone in making fire and wave
Find meeting-place, for flesh and future meet,
The seal in the green wave like you in me,
Child.   My blood at night full of your dreams,
Sleep coming by day as strong as sun on me,
Coming with sun-dreams where leaves and rivers meet,
And I at last alive sunlight and wave.

IX.

Rider of dream, the body as an image
Alone in crisis.   I have seen the wind

Its tall cloud standing on a pillar of air,
The toe of the whirlwind turning on the ground.
Have known in myself hollow bodiless shade,
The shadow falling from the tree to the ground,
Have lost and lost and now at last am found
For a moment of sleep and waking, striking root.

Praise that the homeless may in their bodies be
A house that time makes, where the future moves
In his dark lake.   Praise that the cities of men,
The fields of men, may at all moments choose.
Lose, use, and live.   And at this daylight, praise
To the grace of the world and time that I may hope
To live, to write, to see my human child.

ଏ VII.
From ONE LIFE ଏ

ᕯ ARE YOU BORN?—I ᕯ

A man riding on the meaning of rivers
Sang to me from the cloud of the world:
Are you born?   Are you born?
My name is gone into the burning heart
That knows the change deep in the form of things.
—I saw from the treeline all our cities shine.

A woman riding on the moon of ocean
Sang to me through the cloud of the world:
Are you born?   Are you born?
The form of growing in leaf and crystal flows,
And in the eyes and rivers of the land.
—From the rock of our sky, I came to recognize.

A voice riding on the morning of air
Sang to me from the cloud of the world:
Are you born?   Are you born?
Bring all the singing home;
There is a word of lightning in the grass.
—I stood alive in the young cloud.

ᕯ FIELDS WHERE WE SLEPT ᕯ

Fields where we slept
Lie underwater now
Clay meadows of nightmare
Beneath the shallow wave.

A tremor of speech
On all lips and all mirrors;
Pink sweater and tornado
Announce dawn's littoral.

South lies evocative
On the fine Negro mouth.
Play of silver in streams
Half lake under.

High on the unplowed red
The waterweeds respond,
Where Sheriff Fever
Ordered me to trial.

Where once hatred and fear
Touched me the branch of death,
I may float waves of making
Hung above my lost field.

Remember they say and Incarnatus Est,
The fire-tailed waves, never forget the eyes
Or the distorted jailers or their kindness
Even while they were torturing Mr. Crystal.

Psalms awake and asleep, remember the manmade
Lake where those barren treecrowns rode.
Where air of curses hung, keel of my calm
Rides our created tide.

❧ POWER NEVER DOMINION ❧

Power never dominion.
Some other power.
Some force flaking in light, avalanches of lilies,
Days and the sun renewed in semen, pure
Among the uncorrupted fires, fire's ancestor,
Forgotten;   worshipped secretly;
Where the vestigial Lucifer regales

Craters of memory; where leans
Some fleshly girl, the shaped stones of desire
Leaping in color at her human cunt.
They will translate this girl.   She will appear
In textbooks as a sacrificed antelope
Guilt running shiny over the short fur.
Ideas of shame did split that throat.
But none of that is true tonight.
The girl was leaning over the crater, I dreamt it,
The shrivelled flowers twisted in her hair,
And jewels budded at her throat.
The girl of choice, remembering the past fires,
Praising the word, the columns in the grove,
Arbor vitae uterinae
Locked by such branches, light in the dense forest,
Praising the world unknown and feeling beat
Among her branches
A human child.
Brambles of sense! and that responding power
Rocking the fulness of time.
Until it shall be, what never was:
River and born and dream.

Canals of music downward serenade
New satin gleams under her haunches;
And, running laterally,
And backwards across ripples,
Passing the lower stairs,
Even above the unforgettable murmur,
The sound of oars.

Body of the splendid, bear me now!
Completed by orbits of unhorséd comets,
The bronze, paternal stars.

• PHANERON •

Whatever roams the air is travelling
Over these griefs, these wars and this good.
Whatever cries and changes, lives and reaches
Across the threshold of sense;   I know the piercing name;
Among my silence, in cold, the birth-cry came.
Salt of these tears whitens my eyelashes.

Whatever plows the body turns to food:
Before my face, flowers, color which is form.
Cries plow the sea and air and turn to birth
Upon the people-sown, people-flowering earth.
A year turns in its crisis.   In its sleep.
Whatever plows our dreams is ours to keep.

Whatever plows our dreams is ours to give:
The threshold rises and changes.
I give, I perceive;
Here are the gifts of day risen at last;
Blood of desire, the riding of belief
Beyond our fury and our silences.

Phaneron—anything over the threshold of sense; a perception
word first used by Charles S. Pierce.

• THE RED BRIDGE, SAN FRANCISCO •

A red bridge fastening this city to the forest,
Telling relationship in a stroke of steel;
Cloud-hung among the mist it speaks the real,
In the morning of need asserts the purest
Of our connections : for the opposites
To call direct, to be the word that goes,

Glowing from fires of thought to thought's dense snows,
Growing among the treason and the threats.

Between the summer strung and the young city,
Linking the stonefall to the treefall slope,
Beyond the old namings of body and mind
A red bridge building a new-made identity:
Communion of love opened to cross and find
Self the enemy, this moment and our hope.

ᗌ "IN YOUR TIME, THERE HAVE BEEN THOSE" ᗌ

In your time, there have been those who spoke clearly
For the moment of lightning.
Were we all brave, but at different times?
Even raped open and split, even anonymous,
They spoke.   They are not forgotten.
But they are.   In late summer;   forgot;   caught at
      cross-purposes,
Interrupted in an hour of purity,
Their lives careening along in the fierce cities,
Through atrocious poverties and magnificence,
The unforgotten, the early gone forgot.

Late daytime, and nothing left to hide but an eye endowed
With the charred, guilty, gouged by war, the raging splendor;
Despised like you, criminal in intent;   sunburnt, in love
      and splendid;
This heart, naked and knocking, going in clouds,
Smoke and a cry of light.
In pain, the voice of pain.   The shadow of your cry.
And never forget : you are magnificent beyond all colors.

& "NO ONE EVER WALKING THIS
OUR ONLY EARTH" &

No one ever walking this our only earth, various, very clouded,
    in our forests, in all the valleys of our early dreams,
No one has ever for long seen any thing in full, not live
As any one river or man has run his changes, child
Of the swarms and sowings.   Death nor the woman, seed
Of the born, all growing, going through the grass.
However deep you have looked into the well of the cradle
Or into any dream or open eyes the grave
While the soul, many-leaved and waiting,
Began to assume another exact flower.
Smoke and smell in the wind, a single life!
However true you tell, you never have told.
And even that is not altogether true.   It changes, we say,
    changes, for yes,
Indeed we all know this, any, any of us, there are secrets known
    to all.

Was it indeed shown you in a flash of journey, the flicker along
    change?
In the fine shadow between the curve of lips, shadow of days
    lengthening,
In the flicker of meaning revealed by many windows;
In the form of the eye, the form of words, of the word;   mean-
    ing that formed
These marvelous genitals, nameless as God;
Or in the informing light behind his dream, and he was dreaming
    of you.
Did his own self escape him, now to reach us, reaving the edge
    of cloud?

Has a gift then been given, each other giving our lives?
As air is given to the mouth of all?

ε➤ "MURMURS FROM THE EARTH
OF THIS LAND" ε➤

Murmurs from the earth of this land, from the caves and craters,
    from the bowl of darkness.   Down watercourses of our
    dragon childhood, where we ran barefoot.
We stand as growing women and men.   Murmurs come down
    where water has not run for sixty years.
Murmurs from the tulip tree and the catalpa, from the ax of
    the stars, from the house on fire, ringing of glass;   from
    the abandoned iron-black mill.
Stars with voices crying like mountain lions over forgotten colors.
Blue directions and a horizon, milky around the cities where the
    murmurs are deep enough to penetrate deep rock,
Trapping the lightning-bird, trapping the red central roots.
You know the murmurs.   They come from your own throat.
You are the bridges to the city and the blazing food-plant green;
The sun of plants speaks in your voice, and the infinite shells of
    accretion
A beach of dream before the smoking mirror.
You are close to that surf, and the leaves heated by noon, and
    the star-ax, the miner's glitter walls.   The crests of the sea
Are the same strength you wake with, the darkness is the eyes
    of children forming for a blaze of sight and soon, soon,
Everywhere your own silence, who drink from the crater, the
    nebula, one another, the changes of the soul.

ε➤ ARE YOU BORN?—II ε➤

A child riding the stormy mane of noon
Sang to me past the cloud of the world:
Are you born?   Are you born?
The form of this hope is the law of all things,
Our foaming sun is the toy of that force.

—Touch us alive, developing light!   Today,
Revealed over the mountains, every living eyes.

Child of the possible, who rides the hour
Of dream and process, lit by every fire.
Glittering blood of song, a man who changed
And hardly changed, only flickered, letting pass
A glint of time, showers of human meanings
Flashing upon us all : his story and his song.
The song of a child;   the song of the cloud of the world,
Born, born, born.   Cloud become real,   and change,
The starry form of love.

&∞ VIII.
From BODY OF WAKING &∞

HAYING BEFORE STORM

This sky is unmistakable.   Not lurid, not low, not black.
Illuminated and bruise-color, limitless, to the noon
Full of its floods to come.   Under it, field, wheels, and mountain,
The valley scattered with friends, gathering in
Live-colored harvest, filling their arms;   not seeming to hope
Not seeming to dread, doing.
                                        I stand where I can see
Holding a small pitcher, coming in toward
The doers and the day.
                              These images are all
Themselves emerging : they face their moment : love or go
     down.
A blade of the strong hay stands like light before me.
The sky is a torment on our eyes, the sky
Will not wait for this golden, it will not wait for form.
There is hardly a moment to stand before the storm.
There is hardly time to lay hand to the great earth.
Or time to tell again what power shines past storm.

A BIRTH

Lately having escaped three-kinded death
Not by evasion but by coming through
I celebrate what may be true beginning.
But new begun am most without resource
Stupid and stopped.   How do the newborn grow?
I am of them.   Freshness has taken our hearts;
Pain strips us to the source, infants of further life
Waiting for childhood as we wait for form.

So came I into the world of all the living
The maimed triumphant middle of my way

Where there is giving needing no forgiving.
Saw now the present that is here to say:
Nothing I wrote is what I must see written,
Nothing I did is what I now need done.—
The smile of darkness on my song and my son.

Lately emerged I have seen unfounded houses,
Have seen spirits not opened, surrounded as by sun,
And have, among limitless consensual faces
Watched all things change, an unbuilt house inherit
Materials of desire, that stone and wood and air.
Lit by a birth, I defend dark beginnings,
Waste that is never waste, most-human giving,
Declared and clear as the mortal body of grace.
Beginnings of truth-in-life, the rooms of wilderness
Where truth feeds and the ramifying heart,
Even mine, praising even the past in its pieces,
My tearflesh beckoner who brought me to this place.

≥ MOTHER GARDEN'S ROUND ≥

The year was river-throated, with the stare of legend,
Then truth the whirlwind and Mother Garden.   Death.
And now these stars, antlers, the masks of speech,
And the one ghost a glove in the middle of the floor.
          Garden my green may grow.

If you were here tonight, my heart would rest,
Would rest on a support, happy thereon.
Something is dancing on leafdrift, dancing across the graves:
A child is watching while the world breaks open.
          Garden my green may grow.

Speed of a red fox running along this street.
Everyone could have seen it, no one is now awake.

Separations all year and the seeking of roots.
It was a lie, Mother Garden, they do not wish for death.
             Garden my green may grow.

They wish only to live again.   No more the whirlwind.
One colored pebble now, one look, the singular
Opening of the lips;   a leaf happens to speak.
I remember in love you walked to me straight across the room.
             Garden my green may grow.

The suffering of your absence flies around me now,
No house can keep out this flying of small birds.
Feathers, bird-feathers, settle upon my waking.
The agonies are open.   Faces, dead within them; and on these faces
And filling the clefts and on my hands and eyes
The little fresh pain flutters.   Whitening the grass,
Snowing through the windows.   Drifting over the floor.
Touching my face when, almost, touch means kindness.
My dear dream, Mother Garden.   We wish to be born again.
             Death death may my green grow.

❧ AFTER THEIR QUARREL ❧

After the quarrel in the house I walked the grasses of the field
Until the hissing of breakers and the hissing on the sand
Lowered, and I could see the seed heads and the sky.

A pod of the milkweed burst;   it was speaking to me:
Never mind, never mind.   All splits open.   There is new inside,
We witness.   Downwind, the softened asters let me see

A lengthened sky in its mixed oranges of sunset
Gone east and west, glazing the first bare branches.
The branches said : We know you. I remembered a tiger

The winter I was five not leaping in my dream but fusing
All my wishes to run, with his endless glowing look telling:
I recognize you. Kill them if they deny;   or wake them. Now wake!

Autumn announcing birds, the flights calling from sunset.
One bird crying : I see you down there, bird! The quick furry
   ground
Moves with me in small animals whispering:
You are like us, too.   And the stars.   —I my own evidence

That even the half-eaten and accursed can be a season.
Search yourself, said all the field, understand growth.
When lack consents to leave its seed, waste opens, you will see
Even there, the husband of the spring, who knows his time.

෨ NIGHT FEEDING ෨

Deeper than sleep but not so deep as death
I lay there dreaming and my magic head
remembered and forgot.   On first cry I
remembered and forgot and did believe.
I knew love and I knew evil:
woke to the burning song and the tree burning blind,
despair of our days and the calm milk-giver who
knows sleep, knows growth, the sex of fire and grass,
renewal of all waters and the time of the stars
and the black snake with gold bones.

Black sleeps, gold burns;   on second cry I woke
fully and gave to feed and fed on feeding.
Gold seed, green pain, my wizards in the earth
walked through the house, black in the morning dark.
Shadows grew in my veins, my bright belief,
my head of dreams deeper than night and sleep.

Voices of all black animals crying to drink,
cries of all birth arise, simple as we,
found in the leaves, in clouds and dark, in dream,
deep as this hour, ready again to sleep.

ᨘ THE WATCHERS ᨘ

for Carson and Reeves
She said to me, He lay there sleeping
Upon my bed cast down
With all the bitterness dissolved at last,
An innocent peace within a sleeping head;
He could not find his infant war, nor turn
To that particular zoo, his family of the dead.
I saw her smile of power against his deep
Heart, his waking heart,
Her enmity, her sexual dread.

He said to me, She slept and dreaming
Brought round her face
Closer to me in silence than in fire,
But smiled, but smiled, entering her dark life
Whose hours I never knew, wherein she smiles.
Wherein she dim descending breathes upon
My daylight and the color of waking goes.
Deep in his face, the wanderer
Bringing the gifts of legend and the wars,
Conspiracy of opposing images.

In the long room of dream I saw them sleep,
Turned to each other, clear,
With an obliterated look—
Love, god of foreheads, touching then
Their bending foreheads while the voice of sleep

Wept and sang and sang again
In a chanting of fountains,
A chattering of watches,
Love, sang my sleep, the wavelight on the stone.
I weep to go beyond this throne and the waterlight,
To kiss their eyelids for the last time and pass
From the delicate confidence of their sly throats,
The conversation of their flesh of dreams.
And though I weep in my dream,
When I wake I will not weep.

ह F. O. M. हं

                                    the death of Matthiessen
It was much stronger than they said.   Noisier.
Everything in it more colored.   Wilder.
More at the center calm.
Everything was more violent than ever they said,
Who tried to guard us from suicide and life.
We in our wars were more than they had told us.
Now that descent figures stand about the horizon,
I have begun to see the living faces,
The storm, the morning, all more than they ever said.
Of the new dead, that friend who died today,
Angel of suicides, gather him in now.
Defend us from doing what he had to do
Who threw himself away.

THE SIXTH NIGHT : WAKING

That first green night of their dreaming, asleep beneath the Tree,
God said, "Let meanings move," and there was poetry.

THE BIRTH OF VENUS

Risen in a
welter of waters.

Not as he saw her
standing upon a frayed and lovely surf
clean-riding the graceful leafy breezes
clean-poised and easy.   Not yet.

But born in a
tidal wave of the father's overthrow,
the old rule killed and its mutilated sex.

The testicles of the father-god, father of fathers,
sickled off by his son, the next god Time.
Sickled off.   Hurled into the ocean.
In all that blood and foam,
among raving and generation,
of semen and the sea born, the
great goddess rises.

                However, possibly,
on the long worldward voyage flowing,
horror gone down in birth, the curse, being changed,
being used, is translated far at the margin into
our rose and saving image, curling toward a shore
early and April, with certainly shells, certainly blossoms.

And the girl, the wellborn goddess, human love—
young-known, new-knowing, mouth flickering, sure eyes—
rides shoreward, from death to us as we are at this moment, on the crisp delightful Botticellian wave.

SUITE FOR LORD TIMOTHY DEXTER

I.

They face us in sea-noon sun, just as he saw them waiting,
Bolted down, fastened together by their nailhead proverbs.
The sun still pouring all male all female through their blood
And away through the salt marsh and the white salt sand
Sea-blaze over their shoulders, fantasy
A blue invisible mountain up whose side
Laughter and sharp clouds race as he saw them ride
In whiteness when he as a boy walked down
With morning for a sign.
Smelling of acid, like his trade.
Ready to throw their lifeday down their throats like wine,
Death-rotten proverbs and the jokes all made,
Himself the wine-bottle burning in the sun.

More here than power over proverbs. But that power pours here.
And the sure sun of story, on top the live gold mast.
What's strong, what's lost? What boy walked salty in the light?
A raging worshipping fantastic man,
Tasting money and words, live-breasted women,
The tanner's boy streaked with truth. In the young States
He saw young morning. Wild he was.
And most
A clap of mockery clean in the sea-brightness,
A legend of this coast.

II. How to Impress Massachusetts

A name's a name but
Nothing's the same,
Now King-No-More knows
Lady-No-More;
There may be shame but
He's Mr. Guilt, and
Hell is Mr. War.
The wooden golden eagle
Announces from the rooftree:
Miss Equal, Mr. E.,
Dr. and Mrs. Eden, and
I am Miss Liberty.
But we see Timothy,
No more the colonized,
Look around after labor.
Not a single neighbor
Gives him his due acclaim.
Timothy's surprised:
A harsh laugh, a short knife,
Started his prodigious life.
But he took hold of fate,
Invested in the State, with
Money not worth a damn.
"I," he said, "am what I am,
What's to be done will be done,
The capital will be Washington.
Mr. Hamilton keeps his word,
This country's bond's as sound as me,
Timothy.
What 'dyou say?
'Sound as I'—?
Very well; me is I,
I the tree
Flourishing."
Mr. Hamilton truly meant
An almost infinite per cent

The tanner's boy,
after we become
the United States,
invests in our
currency, which
is generally
regarded as
worthless;

Would accrue
Quickly to
The trustful and the nourishing.
The newborn Federal bank has stirred.   becomes rich,
Timothy is a sword.
A sword without blessing,
A sword without fame,
A sword bearing no signal name.
If Newburyport
Will be blind,
Will seem bored,
Never mind.   and acquires
New Hampshire's kind, and   his new
Calls him "Lord."   first name.
Apprentice then, on the road
Next day wore his freedom suit,
Brided widow and won his house,
Ground their proverbs underfoot.
A poor boy made and found
And funding came to his own tune.
"Lord" is the center of that sound,
And all the songs proclaim
He is the bright blue morning rhyme,
A great name rides before his name.
Turn, burn, and overturn!
Among the squarest houses, he
Is more than Timothy,
And more than merry.
Can forever now retort
Very much Newbury-
Port:
The voice of the people and I can't help it,
But all's easy and no bones broken,
All is well, all in Love.
The first Lord of the age has spoken.
Now all the torment Massachusetts bore
Triumphs in a blaze of love.
Love, love, fantasy,

For
Out of shame and poverty,
From oppression, commerce, war,
Rose a new sovereignty:
The states are free and trade is free
And Dexter's Lord Timothy.

III. Three Nights I Dreamed

Sharp clouds and a sea-moon sang to me
Where were you born my young my dear
I said nowhere vary your singing
Now where was your mother shaded, they sang,
Nowhere I answered the ring the rung
Dark bells rang and I was young —
O on the water then, wine on the sea —
Nowhere they cried and they sang to me —
Nowhere my dear my darling,
My dearly darling beware.

He makes his fortune as a merchant:

Where and nowhere and then the singing changed
Past hills of prophecy the words went ranging,
The colors of the words to images
Went formed.   And all I saw was warming-pans,
Three nights of warming-pans until I woke
And a great ship's bare spars sailing my window,
Up to my tall room window a ship's spars,
And I remembered all the nights and wars,
Sang in my waking of poverty and dream:
My dearly darling beware.

selling warming-pans in the West Indies,

The sun all male and female through me poured,
Awake I bought a cargo all of dream,
Warming-pans for the South, to all the roaring
Nothing, to those who mock at my song.
I have entrusted south my folly cargo,
A full hold coming home now showers gold.

where they are snapped up for molasses-ladles;

165 ⁊

My warming-pans sailed gently to Jamaica —
Rum, rum, my darling beware.

Gold I am, lord of the cats of gold,
Mittens and kittens and coals of gold,
Malta, the Baltic, the Caribbee,
And Britain commend their money to me
As I go funding among the dreamers,
Among their golden nightmares ringing
Among their proverbs a wine-gold bell,
Sounding a folly my dear my darling
My dearly darling dream well.

And then, to spite
their business
sayings, cats to
Malta; mittens
north; and
finally, coals
to Newcastle.

IV. Kings and Contemporaries

How can I speak to them today? What can I know,
What can I show so that we see ourselves?
Voices of stinted singing in the towns,
Voices of wildness and fear of wilderness.
The rhythm, the root.   Gathering in
Sources of music and the wild sea-rose.

Sea-music and the sea building its waters,
The weathervane beast.   My song.

Whenever I say what I mean
They mock and call me mad.
They slip my meaning —
When I mock at them, I
always make money —
How can this go on?
Harum scarum, merchant marum,
My house is built, and my wall of pillars,
A noted house to the Isles of Shoals.
My kings, my presidents, stand round:
I speak in images so they may know
My gold spread-eagle on the cupalow.

*   *   *

Dr. Franklin, Mr. Hamilton, John Hancock, Rufus King,
John Jay, two grenadiers.
Four lions, and here the roof runs so,
That a lamb can lie down with one of the lions,
And an eagle on the cupalow.

He sets up,
around his
house, the
figures of
those he
most admires.

One unicorn, one dog, one horse,
And in the Garden Adam and Eve —
I will if I please have Adam and Eve.
If no man murders me summer or snow
I'll carry this to its fair concluding
With an eagle on the cupalow.

Three of the apostles, viz.
St. Paul St. Peter and St. John.
Venus, Hiram, and Solomon —
The President's platform and columns grow —
I meant marble, but wood it is,
And an eagle on the cupalow.

The Royal Arch,
with lifesize
painted figures
carved by Joseph
Wilson, the
figurehead
sculptor.

George Third, L'Ouverture,
Lord Nelson Baron of the Nile.
Constantinople's Grand Signior,
All heroes, each one in his style—
The Chief Cornplanter with his bow,
His moccasins, arrows, and tomahawk,
And an eagle on the cupalow.

*   *   *

Black rum and silver gin,
Drink for this company.

For the resident poet, Jonathan Plummer,
With a wheelbarrow full of broadsides and haddock —
Malaga wine for Madam Hooper,
Timothy Dexter's fortune-teller;

And for brandy-breasted Lucy, Lucy Lancaster,
Daughter of Princes in Africa,
Feathers and majesty — what for her?
Black rum and silver gin
And a coach with cream-color horses.

Filisy, folosy, silver gin,
Stingalum, stangalum, wine for day,
Ram pan, muski dan,
And wine for night on the sound blind sea.
Stingalum, stangalum, buck.

Rum, whalerbone, whackerbone,
Waterfront, turnpike, Merrimack bridge,
Sea-berry, sea-gold, pine-forest edge;
Wire, briar, limber lock,
Timothy's a red red rock
Surrounded by waves of whisky and wine,
Loving waves called Jonathan,
Lucy Lancaster, Madam Hooper,
And a coach with cream-color horses.

V. The Pickle; The Temple

THE PICKLE

I will say what I mean here;   in a book;
I wants to make
My Enemies grin
Like a cat over
A hot puddin.

If you can bear the truth
Then I will tell the truth:
Man's the best animal,
And the worst —
All men, I say, are more or
Less the Devil's.

From A *Pickle For
the Knowing Ones*,
Timothy Dexter's book.

168 ੈ

Odds make the difference
And there's a sight of odds.
Some half, some quarters.
Odds make the difference.
I see in all places God, the God
Of nature in all things.
We live and move in God,
We live in God.

*   *   *

When great powers ruled,
I was born.
In a snowstorm, the signs
In the seventh house.
Mars came forward
Holding the candle —
Jupiter stood by.
I was to be
One great man.
(I think I am a Quaker
But have so little sense
I can't deceive.)
The bubble is the soul . . .
Man is the giant toad . . .
I have thoughts about clocks
Nobody will believe.
Ask me and I will tell.

*Of his birth
and becoming.*

*   *   *

Now turn the system of knowledge
Into light —
Parents and masters begin, begin schoolmasters
At Cadameys and Collegeys,
Begin ministers,
Leave off, scarecrows in courage,
Brave good apelets —
One thing masters must teach:
Have good manners

169 ह⋗

To parents and people in streets,
And don't be too nosey.
I recommend a school
Of languages,
Scholars to go to
Far parts to trade —
Go supercargo
To learn navigation
And character.
There will in time take
Many brave men,
Advantage to merchants
And funding to country —
Wise men pos-pos on this.
Goodbye — Timothy Dexter.

A plan for
the young:

*   *   *

I command peace and the
Gratest brotherly love
And Not fade, be linked
Together with that best of troue Love
So as to govern all nasions
On the fass of the gloub
Not to
Tiranize over them
But to
Put them to order . . .
A Congress of nasions
To be allways in france
All Despouts is
To be there settled
And this way be Dun
This will balless power
And then all was Dun
A Way — there-for I have the Lam
To Lay Dow with the Lion
Now this may be dun

A Congress of Nations;

If the powers would
A geray to Lay whats called
Devel to one side.

* * *

I being a man without learning

His appeal.

Please to give me Light.

* * *

The knowing ones complain
Of my book
The first edition
Had no stops
I put in a Nuf here
And they may peper
And solt it as they plese
,,,,,,,,, ,,,,,,,,,
,,,,,,,,, ,,,,,,,,,
········· ·········
,,,,,,,,,,,,,,,,,,,,
······!!!!!!!!!!······
·······!!!!!!!·······
·········!!!·········
··········!··········
,,,,,,,,,,,,,,,,,,,,,,,
····??????????····

THE TEMPLE

Then with a touch of the gout, and being
A little sober in the morning
I raised in the garden a Temple of Reason
For my own funeral,
Furnished with pipes and tobacco, a speaking trumpet
And fireworks in the tomb,
A Bible to read, and some good songs.
I sent out invitations.

He holds his
own funeral,

Now it was time to begin.

It was a fine clear day,
I had fine pallbearers
Lord East Lord West Lord North and Lord South
Lord Megul and Lord Shambow.
The minister made his prayer —
Doctor Strong, he was —
And the flimsy sextons were there
And very much crying.
About 3000 came,
Oh, half the town, I'd say.
The procession wound   *and watches from*
Under my window   *an upper window.*
Across the garden to my
Temple of Reason.
My coffin was long ready,
Painted in my house.
White lead inside
And outside touched with green.
Noble trimmings, eight handles
And an uncommon lock.
Now it was put into the
Temple of Reason.
Out in the kitchen I was
Beating my wife;
The ghostly lady
Had hardly mourned at all.

Very few people
Should attend funerals.
Many catch cold, and we
Want to settle Ohio;
We can't spare these beauties
To die so soon.

VI. The Kind of Woman

Ghostly in my house
A woman I married —

Ghostly up the stairs,
Like snow in the hall.
At midnight in her bed
The ghostly-breasted;
I cannot have her ghost
Walking my palace.
They say she is alive.
I say she will ever be
Mrs. Dexter that was.
The attacks of the ghost
Will not let me sleep. —
Now to save my life.

I will sell the house,
Horses, the cream-color horses
And the coach.
If not I will let it.
Wait.   I can sweep my house
And get all anew
And go out of hell.
I will advertise.

"A very colding wife
Is poison to me.
I wish to be still
And master of my cash;
And therefore I wish for
One very good housekeeper.
Them that know me know
The kind of woman.
Now I will say
What kind of a person,
From thirty to forty
And a good jade
That will trot pace and gallop—
Not to heave one off
But, rather of the two,
Heave on. —I mean right well.

He is haunted by
his living wife.

"I must have a
Companion four
good by all."

173 ॐ

Now stop, I got off the path;
Now I am honest : I wish for
A middling woman for size,
Sensible honest and comely,
Knowing when to speak
And when to be silent,
With a nose like mine."

VII. Guessing Time

A feat of laughter and a coastwise dance
Among the ills of ocean, in pauper light
Imagining truth, at dawn turning from madness
Into the unknown world, up blue invisible
Mountains of fantasy climbing
To the sea.
Where he as a boy walked down, salty, in brightness
Raging and worshipping.
Their faces turn again the nailhead stare
Of proverbs glaring at the intuitive.
My old head has
Worn out three bodies.
Amen.   Clean truth.
Pay the whole debt, it will make nations tremble.
Keep up to what we set out to be, honest republicans,
No king, but you won't go it long without being honest;
If dishonest, you must have a king.
Keep Judas out of your councils.
Watch day and night, for mankind is mankind.
Jockey-handed priests, deacons, grunters, whiners —
(And I will show you one more private torture:
Abraham Bishop my son-in-law from whom
I live in hell on earth;   pity me, fellow mortals,
A.B. mad with learning, as poor as a snake,
As proud as Lucifer.   A.B. is a beast,
A Connecticut bull, short neck, thick curly hair.
When I see my father, the great good man,
Father Thomas Jefferson, he'll shed great tears with grief.)

A sortment, a sortment is good in a shop.

How many nicknames three things have:
Sex and glory and the grave.

Now I suppose I may guess
As it is guessing time:
I guess the world is all one
Very large living creature;
Mankind is the master beast,
As in the sea the whale
Is head fish — master over the
Whole of beasts and fish,
But still we're all one creature.
Man is the masterly beast,
And also the worst of the whole,
Knowing the most and acting the worst
According to what we know.

I think when the candle goes out
Men and women are done at one blow,
We will lie then as dirt of rocks
Until the great gun go —
9,000,000,000 tons
Of the best good powder.
That will shake and bring all the
Bones together,
Then the world will be to an end.
All kinds of music then,
And funding laid aside,
The melody will be very great, —
Now why won't you believe me?

It is true as apple-seed,
The sea and sea-music.
True as the voices that through me burn —
As true as we died and we are born,
Apple-seed and apple-thorn

Calling root and calling hand,
Saying Amen, mockery, Amen, fantasy,
Sea-music and the sea.

❧ VOICES OF WAKING ❧

                for the eightieth birthday of Frances G. Wickes
Whenever you wake, you will find journeying —
Even in deep night, dreams surrounding your dreams —
The song of waking begun, prepared in silence,
Planted in silence as her life is planted
Among the constellations and the days.

Whenever you wake, you will hear entering
The song of meanings, a melody of green;
The image of a legendary woman
Dancing among her mercies, in essence emerging
Female to leap into the dragon-thronging sea.

Voices of nourishing, lifting the newborn up,
Away, —they lift away, newborn to all,
To the nourisher, to self born, to new life.
Voices of waking that journey in our lives
As renaissance and rain of images.

All of the people of the play are here,
In a storm of light;   birthday;   at any moment.
Full in their powers, and the voice of waking
Sings for beginnings;   she sings, wherever waking is.
Wherever the deep moon stands, the song arrives.
Nevertheless the moon goes voyages.

Nevertheless, the journeying is time:
Makes birthdays, makes this birthday a resonance

And the remote boundaries of imagining
Acknowledge the voices, her daily human voice,
Blessing this birthday moment her monument.

Deep in the waking, her life builds in light
The vision of the body of the soul.

❧ BODY OF WAKING ❧

Fire-thread in the valley.   Bird-voice in darkness.
Before the opening of the world.   In our own time.
Days we then heard the cities in their singing,
Armies standing in their graves imagining certain mornings,
Hours a naked man in the stream high on the mountain
Imagined this, too, among the cold water,
Looking up at the forming sky.

Century of absence in the valley of confusion.

When you wake, even startled awake, even in shadowless night,
      even alone, the song
Will be growing.   The song begun will be growing in fiery
      night;   in blackness, voices
Pouring over the unseen cities, and the mountains wake,
Riverlands unseen, immediacy of song.

*

Century of absence.   It could be like a time
When the soul that has slept leaps from its priests,
Spring when the old idea is at last available to all children,
And God in the world is on the lips of love.
Hot out of the dried blood of the separate churches,
The nations, separate wards in the same hospital.
Revenge which spikes the cross and splits the star

Withers the crescent.   The world circles among
The solitude of Spain, the solitude of Stalingrad,
Solitude in the hills of loess and the caves of Africa,
And now your solitude, New York, who raised yourself above.

Now the buried questions flicker on all faces.
Does the fat belly know its heart is broken?
Do you drag yourself through the wilderness saying
Never mind how we got here;   that will come later?
Much later, after you speak of the weapon birds
And the spies in your milk and the little split children
Bleeding models of cars;   you told their fortunes
According to a harvest of slot-machines;
According to the obscene pattern of bombers.
Much later, after you glare for eight days, silent,
After you howl for a century and a half,
You look at the clock and see it has not moved.
What do you do then?   Weep for the generations?
You change your life.   No.   You begin again
Going on from the moment in which you stand today.
Will there be suffering?   Perhaps not as much as now.
But will there be suffering, in the healing?   Yes.
Only with a difference.   You will know it then.
Walking down Basin Street, will be aware.
And that, my darling, my dear dear, is what Mother prays for,
Beside the cradle, lighting the candles of the days,
In retreat, in the kitchen, watching by living bodies
And waiting endlessly by the unmoving face
While the door is still not, not really, not yet, opened.
My darling, my baby, my people, my own self.

The words rising from the sleep of America:
I had all my children, and they locked themselves in,
My babies are sick to death, and the doctor is not well.
Ruddy we are, strong we are, and insane.
They built doors around themselves, and then they locked the
    doors.
Some believe they are doctors.   Some believe they are patients,
Some think they are statisticians.   Some are ambassadors.

We eat very well.   We keep the pictures on.
Sometimes the clocks jump fifty minutes.   Some days they do
    not move.
Some play they are parents.   Some always are the children.
We are careful to flush the toilet.   We sleep well.
Of course it's a toilet.   Of course it's a swimming pool.

The force that split the spirit could found a city,
That held the split could shine the lights of science.
This rigid energy could still break and run dancing
Over the rockies and smokies of all lives.
How many moons circle our dreams?   America,
Did you think only of wars and luxury?
Can you remember your early dreaming?

Who of us fully living
Among these inward murders,
Among the ritual
Of domination?

I remember the structure of towers
Torches over New York
I remember the structure of crystals
A single sheet of flow
I know an immortal journey
And we all walk hypnotized by a cliff
Speed and explosion.

Voices of process, river of human meanings.
Put your hand in, come into the dance,
Turn around fine, take out your hand,
Dance yourself once.
You know this music.
You were born among these songs.

Now we tell, sing, and relate.
The buried life and the body of waking.

*

Bird-voice in darkness.   Tremor of night moving.
The rocks accept blackness.   Now I remember trees.
Across the crystals of time forming I suddenly feel
The flow of a cold breeze following a bird-voice
The river remade, the invitation of water
Moving in praise of process.
In time the river turns, in time turn the wakers
Among their colored dreams,
In time our frightful processions
May turn toward morning and turn toward form.

Now the praise of the moving into light,
The melody of this walking, the broken breathing even of us
Who moved to discover the children in the forest,
The children of our own dreams who would save us.
Even among our broken failing years
And the acts to bind us, the look between two faces,
Ways and grace,
The melody of praise and the whisper of green
Before the opening of the world,
In our own time.
That was long before we knew what was required,
Before we began ever to hear the questions.

But the young, talking together of growth and form,
Arrived once more at the terms.   In praise of process,
Our songs were, of the seed;   we took the joy
Of the eye dancing unborn, its precise fore-lighting
Moving in unborn dark toward the achieved gaze,
Seeking continually developing light.
Seeking as we began to grow, and resting without distrust,
We moved toward a requirement still unknown.

We spoke of the heroes, the generous ones, who gave their mean-
     ings,
Knowing again meaning as music,
Meaning in all its moving, as process, as song,
As the enlightened seed transformed in dark and light.

Color transformed us.　　We knew the dance of selves,
Growing, meaning giving us our green.
And toward a future the music goes.

Flashing of meaning as the light we breathe,
And through the whole night moving, coming as music.
Music that grows in silence, along dark a single voice
On its long stair of sound going up darkness
Moving toward form, moving becoming meaning
That makes our sleeping.
　　　　　　　　　　Silent
Until the river under the voice discovers
Its own currents, a flowing in a stream.
While air follows its own music.

Throat of song.　　The air-achieving bird
Sings in the blackness.
Hours past midnight and a throat of music,
The dark night offering.
Fleet of voices in a single turning
Stair of calling and the flying pauses
Go as darkness and grow as constellations.
Voices of all music going toward its form
In human meanings and in silences.
Arriving again as the weather of our days
Over born water, on waking faces.
Growing to feed each other, lover, mother of gesture
To turn against fear and withholden reach,
The movement at the center of all things
Making a stillness never a refusal.
Dream and creation and sea,
Violent precise act,
Movement to match our lives,
Wish at the center of growth
We feel as peace.
Peace the love of the process of our lives
For the movement at the center of all things.

Voice diving deep.
Deep in the lights of silence.
When night no longer imagines sunlight,
And we going darker come to all music,
Deep in the clearoscure, where we alone
And all alone go through the texture of time
To the flowing present that becomes all things,
The energy of myth and star and bone.

Now the heroes of process
Not leaders but lives
Is even the lost girl walking the length of the forest
Even the child whose January wrists
Stuck out below his blowing sleeves.　　Weeping, he was,
Along the avenue.　　And the man who faced the spies
At the Segre River.　　Long ago.　　In Spain.

Another image of the born, the next woman,
Another image of the next power of man
Finds itself dreaming in the world of form.
Entering, long before we enter,
The new requirement, the world of morning.

*

Here's day beginning, the blessed, the unbegun, the song, the
　　given.
For that the human wish to grow acts through his giving
The living will be giving you your doors and apples.
Self torn from its old lies, walking and eating,
Becoming music and bone,
All incomplete without the rest
And peaceful over time
No longer cruel in partial truth,
Knowledge of giving and taking
Enters now and lets us live.
Lets us arrive at the present when the world
Has the choice of each of us, to make life or suicide,
To give or die.

*

They have eluded us.   They are not here.
Statues turning to cloud among the music
Float overhead, promising rain and seasons
In the black, the day in midnight.
Dayray before the way.
Rides on a flickering breath, the changes of darkness,
Exchange of murders.   Bodies exchanging life.
Where the belief flows somewhere
Uncorrupt, hidden, under violence,
Making its own and dawn-announcing act,
River of daybreak, where the waking is,
Still to be sung among the deaths and days.

These meanings become the light we breathe,
The breathing of a theme;   in our own time.

&> IX.
WATERLILY FIRE &>

THE SPEAKING TREE

for Robert Payne
Great Alexander sailing was from his true course turned
By a young wind from a cloud in Asia moving
Like a most recognizable most silvery woman;
Tall Alexander to the island came.
The small breeze blew behind his turning head.
He walked the foam of ripples into this scene.

The trunk of the speaking tree looks like a tree-trunk
Until you look again.   Then people and animals
Are ripening on the branches;   the broad leaves
Are leaves;   pale horses, sharp fine foxes
Blossom;   the red rabbit falls
Ready and running.   The trunk coils, turns,
Snakes, fishes.   Now the ripe people fall and run,
Three of them in their shore-dance, flames that stand
Where reeds are creatures and the foam is flame.

Stiff Alexander stands.   He cannot turn.
But he is free to turn : this is the speaking tree,
It calls your name.   It tells us what we mean.

TO ENTER THAT RHYTHM
WHERE THE SELF IS LOST

To enter that rhythm where the self is lost,
where breathing : heartbeat : and the subtle music
of their relation make our dance, and hasten
us to the moment when all things become
magic, another possibility.
That blind moment, midnight, when all sight
begins, and the dance itself is all our breath,
and we ourselves the moment of life and death.

Blinded;   but given now another saving,
the self as vision, at all times perceiving,
all arts all senses being languages,
delivered of will, being transformed in truth —
for life's sake surrendering moment and images,
writing the poem;   in love making;   bringing to birth.

ঌ THE WAY OUT, *from* "AKIBA" ঌ

The night is covered with signs.   The body and face of man,
    with signs, and his journeys.   Where the rock is split
    and speaks to the water;   the flame speaks to the cloud;
    the red splatter, abstraction, on the door
    speaks to the angel and the constellations.
The grains of sand on the sea-floor speak at last to the noon.
And the loud hammering of the land behind
    speaks ringing up the bones of our thighs, the hoofs,
    we hear the hoofs over the seethe of the sea.

All night down the centuries, have heard, music of passage.

Music of one child carried into the desert;
    firstborn forbidden by law of the pyramid.
Drawn through the water with the water-drawn people
    led by the water-drawn man to the smoke mountain.
The voice of the world speaking, the world covered by signs,
    the burning, the loving, the speaking, the opening.
Strong throat of sound from the smoking mountain.
Still flame, the spoken singing of a young child.
The meaning beginning to move, which is the song.

Music of those who have walked out of slavery.

Into that journey where all things speak to all things,
    refusing to accept the curse, and taking

for signs, the signs of all things, the world, the body
which is part of the soul, and speaks to the world,
all creation being created in one image, creation.
This is not the past walking into the future,
the walk is painful, into the present, the dance
not visible as dance until much later.
These dancers are discoverers of God.

We knew we had all crossed over when we heard the song.

Out of a life of building lack on lack:
the slaves refusing slavery, escaping into faith:
an army who came to the ocean : the walkers
who walked through the opposites, from I to opened Thou,
city and cleave of the sea.   Those at flaming Nauvoo,
the ice on the great river : the escaping Negroes,
swamp and wild city;   the shivering children of Paris
and the glass black hearses;   those on the Long March:
all those who together are the frontier, forehead of man.

Where the wilderness enters, the world, the song of the world.

Akiba rescued, secretly, in death-windings
by his disciples carried from Jerusalem
to whatever he was loving with his life.
The wilderness journey through which we move
under the whirlwind truth into the new,
the only accurate.   A cluster of lights at night:
faces before the pillar of fire.   A child watching
while the sea breaks open.   This night.   The way in.

Barbarian music, a new song.

Acknowledging opened water, possibility:
open like a woman to this meaning.
In a time of building statues of the stars
valuing certain partial ferocious skills
while past us the chill and immense wilderness

spreads its one-color wings until we know
rock, water, flame, cloud, or the floor of the sea,
the world is a sign, a way of speaking.   To find.
What shall we find?   Energies, rhythms, a journey.

Ways to discover.   The song of the way in.

?❧ FOR A MEXICAN PAINTER ?❧

Carlos, your art is embryos,
These eyes are shaping in the dark;
There is a fate map in this red
Line and that bright red line,
The earliest map of all.

These eyes are shaping in the dark
Toward the requirement of light
And all will grow as they have grown;
Even transplanted will perform
Selfwise, themselves, this one, that one.

Deep in the hieratic blood
Toward sleep toward dream the process goes,
Toward waking move the sex, the heart,
The self as woman man and rose.
Carlos, your art is embryos.

❧ A SONG OF ANOTHER TRIBE ❧

Guilt   said the bony man
Do you feel guilt
At your desires?
No   I said   my guilt comes when
My desires find no way.
Country of sand and claws;
I wait for my rescuer.
No one will venture there.

Out of long silences
Come I to wordless song
O let my singing bring me
To that place
Where live waters
Rise and go.
There may the living arrive,
Go and return.
Find me, and I find,
And go finding.
A beating sound, I hear
A sound of riding.
Speed after silence
And at last music,
Words of another tribe:

My riding is on swift mares,
My love is by the green water-springs;
For a short moment I will sit there,
I will look upon her wandering face,
I will put an end to the black delay.

𐅛 SONG 𐅛

A voice flew out of the river as morning flew
  out of the body of night, a voice sending
  out from the night of the sleeping
Morning : a voice in its own voice, naked, made
  of the whole body and the whole life
But without anything
Breath
Breath of the fire love
Smoke of the poems voices

𐅛 WATERLILY FIRE 𐅛

for Richard Griffith

I. The Burning

Girl grown woman fire mother of fire
I go the stone street turning to fire. Voices
Go screaming Fire to the green glass wall.
And there where my youth flies blazing into fire
The dance of sane and insane images, noon
Of seasons and days. Noontime of my one hour.

Saw down the bright noon street the crooked faces
Among the tall daylight in the city of change.
The scene has walls stone glass all my gone life
One wall a web through which the moment walks
And I am open, and the opened hour
The world as water-garden lying behind it.
In a city of stone, necessity of fountains,
Forced water fallen on glass, men with their axes.

An arm of flame reaches from water-green glass,
Behind the wall I know waterlilies
Drinking their light, transforming light and our eyes
Skythrown under water, clouds under those flowers,
Walls standing on all things stand in a city noon
Who will not believe a waterlily fire.
Whatever can happen in a city of stone,
Whatever can come to a wall can come to this wall.

I walk in the river of crisis toward the real,
I pass guards, finding the center of my fear
And you, Dick, endlessly my friend during storm.

The arm of flame striking through the wall of form.

II. The Island

Born of this river and this rock island, I relate
The changes : I born when the whirling snow
Rained past the general's grave and the amiable child
White past the windows of the house of Gyp the Blood.
General, gangster, child.   I know in myself the island.

I was the island without bridges, the child down
                                    whose blazing
Eye the men of plumes and bone raced their canoes and fire
Among the building of my young childhood, houses;
I was those changes, the live darknesses
Of wood, the pale grain of a grove in the fields
Over the river fronting red cliffs across —
And always surrounding her the river, birdcries, the wild
Father building his sand, the mother in panic her parks —
Bridges were thrown across, the girl arose
From sleeping streams of change in the change city.
The violent forgetting, the naked sides of darkness.
Fountain of a city in growth, an island of light and water.
Snow striking up past the graves, the yellow cry of spring.

Whatever can come to a city can come to this city.

Under the tall compulsion
                        of the past
I see the city
                change like a man changing
I love this man
                with my lifelong body of love
I know you
                among your changes
                                        wherever I go
Hearing the sounds of building
                        the syllables of wrecking
A young girl watching
                        the man throwing red hot rivets
Coals in a bucket of change
How can you love a city that will not stay?
I love you
            like a man of life in change.

Leaves like yesterday shed, the yellow of green spring
Like today accepted and become one's self
I go, I am a city with bridges and tunnels,
Rock, cloud, ships, voices.   To the man where the river met
The tracks, now buried deep along the Drive
Where blossoms like sex pink, dense pink, rose, pink, red.

Towers falling.   A dream of towers.
Necessity of fountains.   And my poor,
Stirring among our dreams,
Poor of my own spirit, and tribes, hope of towers
And lives, looking out through my eyes.
The city the growing body of our hate and love,
The root of the soul, and war in its black doorways.
A male sustained cry interrupting nightmare.
Male flower heading upstream.

Among a city of light, the stone that grows.
Stigma of dead stone, inert water, the tattered
Monuments rivetted against flesh.

194 ❧

Blue noon where the wall made big agonized men
Stand like sailors pinned howling on their lines, and I
See stopped in time a crime behind green glass,
Lilies of all my life on fire.
Flash faith in a city building its fantasies.

I walk past the guards into my city of change.

III. Journey Changes

Many of us   Each in his own life waiting
Waiting to move   Beginning to move   Walking
And early on the road of the hill of the world
Come to my landscapes emerging on the grass

The stages of the theatre of the journey

I see the time of willingness between plays
Waiting and walking and the play of the body
Silver body with its bosses and places
One by one touched awakened into into

Touched and turned one by one into   flame

The theatre of the advancing goddess   Blossoming
Smiles as she stands intensely being in stillness
Slowness in her blue dress advancing standing I go
And far across a field over the jewel grass

The play of the family stroke by stroke acted out

Gestures of deep acknowledging on the journey stages
Of the playings the play of the goddess and the god
A supple god of searching and reaching
Who weaves his strength   Who dances her more alive

The theatre of all animals, my snakes, my great horses

Always the journey   long   patient   many haltings
Many waitings for choice and again easy breathing
When the decision to go on is made
Along the long slopes of choice and again the world

The play of poetry approaching in its solving

Solvings of relations in poems and silences
For we were born to express   born for a journey
Caves, theatres, the companioned solitary way
And then I came to the place of mournful labor

A turn in the road and the long sight from the cliff

Over the scene of the land dug away to nothing and many
Seen to a stripped horizon carrying barrows of earth
A hod of earth taken and emptied and thrown away
Repeated farther than sight.   The voice saying slowly

But it is hell.   I heard my own voice in the words
Or it could be a foundation   And after the words
My chance came.   To enter.   The theatres of the world.

IV. Fragile

I think of the image brought into my room
Of the sage and the thin young man who flickers and asks.
He is asking about the moment when the Buddha
Offers the lotus, a flower held out as declaration.
"Isn't that fragile?" he asks.   The sage answers:
"I speak to you.   You speak to me.   Is that fragile?"

V. The Long Body

This journey is exploring us. Where the child stood
An island in a river of crisis, now
The bridges bind us in symbol, the sea
Is a bond, the sky reaches into our bodies.
We pray : we dive into each other's eyes.

Whatever can come to a woman can come to me.

This is the long body : into life from the beginning,
Big-headed infant unfolding into child, who stretches and finds
And then flowing the young one going tall, sunward,
And now full-grown, held, tense, setting feet to the ground,
Going as we go in the changes of the body,
As it is changes, in the long strip of our many
Shapes, as we range shifting through time.
The long body : a procession of images.

This moment in a city, in its dream of war.
                    We chose to be,
Becoming the only ones under the trees
                              when the harsh sound
Of the machine sirens spoke. There were these two men,
And the bearded one, the boys, the Negro mother feeding
Her baby. And threats, the ambulances with open doors.
Now silence. Everyone else within the walls. We sang.
             We are the living island,
We the flesh of this island, being lived,
Whoever knows us is part of us today.

Whatever can happen to anyone can happen to me.

Fire striking its word among us, waterlilies
Reaching from darkness upward to a sun
Of rebirth, the implacable.   And in our myth
The Changing Woman who is still and who offers.

Eyes drinking light, transforming light, this day
That struggles with itself, brings itself to birth.
In ways of being, through silence, sources of light
Arriving behind my eye, a dialogue of light.

And everything a witness of the buried life.
This moment flowing across the sun, this force
Of flowers and voices body in body through space.
The city of endless cycles of the sun.

I speak to you   You speak to me

❧ NOTES ❧

LIVES. This group of poems will include *Gibbs, Ryder, Chapman, Ann Burlak, Ives, Timothy Dexter, Akiba, Kathe Kollwitz, Bessie Smith,* and *Boas.*

I wish to acknowledge my debt to Horace Gregory and Dr. Theodore Shedlovsky, who first told me about Gibbs; to Marsden Hartley, for his talk about Ryder; to Ives' "Essays Before a Sonata"; to the staff of the Portsmouth Public Library, and to Richardson Wright's and John P. Marquand's books about Timothy Dexter; to Louis Finkelstein's biography, and my mother's story that we were descended from Akiba. *Akiba* has not yet been published in book form; the last three of the *Lives* are not yet published.

ELEGIES. "When the elegy appears, in surviving Greek literature, we find it dedicated, not to death, but to war and love."
—*The Encyclopædia Britannica,* 11th ed.

In the second elegy, there are quotations from *The Sixth Book of Moses,* and from "Peredur" in *The Mabinogion.* The references in the third elegy are to the war in Spain; I went into Catalonia on a quite different errand on the first day, when none of us in England knew there would be war. The "sphere at the joint" was a recommendation made by the artist Charles Biederman, when he saw the first cyclotron at Chicago. The recommendation worked. The seventh elegy uses a paper by Philleo Nash on Revivalism among the Klamath Indians in 1870. It quotes from *Peer Gynt,* and from material from the concentration camps; and the ninth elegy uses Anna Freud's reports. The quotation in the tenth elegy is from Wyatt.

MRS. WALPURGA. Dr. René Dubos saying to me, "Pasteur said, 'La vie, c'est l'œuf et son devenir.'"

WATERLILY FIRE. The time of this poem is tne period in New York City from April, 1958, when I witnessed the destruction of Monet's *Waterlilies* by fire at the Museum of Modern Art, to the present moment.

The two spans of time assumed are the history of Manhattan Island and my lifetime on the island. I was born in an apartment house that had as another of its tenants the notorious gangster Gyp the Blood. Nearby was Grant's Tomb and the grave of the Amiable Child. This child died very young when this part of New York was open country. The place with its memory of amiability has been protected among all the rest. My father, in the building business, made us part of the building, tearing down, and rebuilding of the city, with all that that implies. Part II is based on that time, when building still meant the throwing of red-hot rivets, and only partly the pouring of concrete of the later episodes.

Part IV deals with an actual television interview with Suzuki, the Zen teacher, in which he answered a question about a most important moment in the teachings of Buddha.

The long body of Part V is an idea from India of one's lifetime body as a ribbon of images, all our changes seen in process.

The "island of people" was the group who stayed out in the open in City Hall Park in April of 1961, while the rest of the city took shelter at the warning sound of the sirens. The protest against this nuclear-war practice drill was, in essence, a protest against war itself and an attempt to ask for some other way to deal with the emotions that make people make war.

Before the Museum of Modern Art was built, I worked for a while in the house that then occupied that place. On the day of the fire, I arrived to see it as a place in the air. I was coming to keep an appointment with my friend the Curator of the Museum's Film Library, Richard Griffith, to whom this poem is dedicated.

M. R.

200 ছঌ